ALADDIN

A family pantomime

Further recent titles from LinguaBooks

The Legend of Sidora
In A Strange Land
A Busker on Bow Street
Lost Dreams
The Farmer's Son
The Seasonal Visitor

ALADDIN

A family pantomime

by Roy Byrom

LinguaBooks
www.linguabooks.com

Roy Byrom has asserted his right under the Copyright, Designs and Patents Act, 1988 to be identified as the author of this work.

ISBN: 978-1-911369-34-9

First edition

Editor: Ann Claypole
Proofreader: Marie-Christin Strobel

A CIP catalogue record for this book is available from the British Library.

LinguaBooks
Elsie Whiteley Innovation Centre
Hopwood Lane
Halifax HX1 5ER
www.linguabooks.com

Performance Rights

No performances of this work are permitted without the author's express permission

---

Production and license enquiries should be addressed to:

LinguaBooks
Elsie Whiteley Innovation Centre
Hopwood Lane, Halifax HX1 5ER
United Kingdom
Tel. 01422 399 554
info@linguabooks.com

A licence issued to perform this pantomime does not include permission to use any incidental music specified in the present work. Licensees are solely responsible for obtaining written permission from the respective copyright owners to use copyrighted music and/or lyrics during the performance of this work. Accordingly, licensees are solely responsible and liable for all music clearances and shall indemnify the copyright owners of this work and their publishers and agents against any costs, expenses, losses and liabilities arising from the use of copyrighted music and/or lyrics by licensees.

Billing and credit requirements

All advertising and publicity material (leaflets, programmes, flyers, posters, etc., including any announcement made via digital or social media) relating to any actual or indented production of this work must include the following billing details, each item of which shall be displayed in a prominent form and position:

Aladdin
a family pantomime
by Roy Byrom
in association with LinguaBooks

Foreword

There can be few things more quintessentially British than the panto and Roy Byrom's delightful interpretation of the classic, Aladdin, is a superb contemporary example of the genre. All the traditional elements are cleverly worked into a storyline that skilfully combines old and new comedy routines, favourite gags and contemporary humour with a lavish dose of song and dance, all in the spirit of good, clean family fun.

At its best, a pantomime is not only an opportunity to laugh out loud, cheer the hero or heroine and boo the villain, it is also a cathartic experience. You know you will leave the theatre in high spirits, that evil will succumb to the pure of spirit and that order will be restored. In the words of George Bernard Shaw, 'A child who has never seen a pantomime is a public danger.' More than any other type of live theatrical entertainment, pantos can be enjoyed by young and old and genuinely help to bring generations together. Fashions come and go, musical tastes change radically from one generation to the next and the blockbuster movies enjoyed by one's parents often elicit only a wry smile from their offspring. But panto is here to stay. Where else can you see children, parents and grandparents joining in the fun together, shouting at the top of their voices and immersing themselves in a fantasy world of zany fairy-tale characters and larger-than-life villains?

So what is the secret of the panto's enduring success? Partly it is the very zaniness of the characters combined with a powerful visual and musical spectacle fine-tuned over the years to incorporate everyone's favourite set pieces to stave off the predictability of the outcome till the last minute, but it is also the flexibility and adaptability of the genre. It is an art from that is strict in its structure and concept but knows virtually no bounds in terms of the type of content that can be included. From a musical point of view, anything goes, ballads, rock, jazz, hip hop, grunge or whatever takes the fancy of a contemporary audience. Jokes and gags can draw liberally from other forms of entertainment, but also topical news stories, politics and personalities are fair game for the panto wit. And royalty, of course, has a very special place in the magical world of panto in which emperors and empresses, kings and queens, princes and princesses abound.

As an art form, the British panto is truly unique. It is partly rooted in the Italian Commedia Dell'Arte and similarly features easily recognisable stock characters, but there are French influences, too, mainly through the ballets-pantomimes that were put on in London by visiting French troupes in the second half of the seventeenth century. Similarly, John Rich's eighteenth-century Drury Lane pantomimes combined a folk story with a harlequinade telling the comic adventures of Harlequin, his lover Columbine and her father Pantaloon. And of course, Pierrot, the servant, made his appearance there, too, the forerunner of many a pantomime servant and chief clown. But over the years, these and many other influences morphed into the multi-faceted show we know today, in which the action not only takes place in remote lands, but in which the principal boy is played by a girl and the panto dame by a man. Panto was a world of inclusivity and diversity long before these terms became foremost in the popular consciousness.

Aladdin is a prime example of the best panto tradition and probably the most exotic of them all. The story of the young son of a washerwoman who falls in love with a princess, is locked in a cave by an evil magician, rescued with the help of a genie and eventually wins the heart of the princess contains all the dramatic elements one has come to expect plus a unique mix of locations, cultures, nations and nationalities. Although the story dates from the Arabian Nights (or Thousand and One Nights) and was originally set in Baghdad, British tradition has shifted the main action to Old Peking, and the Sultan of the earlier version has become the Emperor of China. The result is a delightful mixture of Arab and Chinese elements and this is often reflected in the costumes and settings. Roy Byrom's version adds another dimension altogether, taking Aladdin and the audience completely out of this world. I am sure that this script will serve theatre companies well in helping to provide many hours of pure entertainment for theatregoers wherever and whenever it is performed.

Maurice Claypole, 2019

Author's Note

This is a traditional children's family pantomime – with a twist. Poor boy meets rich girl and they fall in love. Boy becomes rich, loses his riches – and the girl. Then all ends happily in the end! All the ingredients are there for you to laugh, shout, boo, clap and have a really good time being transported out of this world where, supposedly, there is no atmosphere. OH YES, THERE IS!!

Productions

This new version of the traditional family pantomime was first performed at Leeds City Varieties.

At the time of publication, production was underway for a run at the Halifax Playhouse commencing 13 December 2019 with the following cast (subject to change):

Aladdin Twanky .... Francesca Foster
Princess Lotus Blossom .... Kerry Lawrance
Widow Twanky ....Stuart Davison
Wishee Washee Twanky ....James Chatburn
Emperor Ying Tong ....Paul Dargan
Empress Ping Pong .... Judith Hardaker
Grand Vizir ....Ian Slim
Prince Pekoe .... Kristina Liddicoat
Abanazer ....Martin Walker
Genie ....Wayne Illingworth
Chop Suey ....Nathan Coulson
Chow Mein .... Luke Beevers
Sing Hi ....Christine Noble Doyle
Sing Lo .... Caitlin Jennings
Executioner .... Wayne Illingworth
2nd Executioner ....Robert Bray
Surprise ....Steve Kell
Fairy Diamante .... Kasha Wolny

Director ....John Eastwood
Assistant director .... Leighton Hirst
Musical Director ....Brian Chapman

Characters

Aladdin Twanky	F	The ambitious Chinese laundry boy
Princess Lotus Blossom	F	A China doll
Widow Twanky	M	Big and beautiful (well big anyway!)
Wishee Washee Twanky	M	Aladdin's cheeky brother
Emperor Ying Tong	M	Mint imperial fallen on hard times
Empress Ping Pong	F	The power behind the throne
Grand Vizir	M	The Prime Minister with great expectations
Prince Pekoe	F	A reluctant suitor
Abanazer	M	A thoroughly nasty piece of work
Genie	M	Flash, bang and magic too!
Chop Suey	M	Reluctant henchman
Chow Mein	M	Reluctant anything!
Sing Hi	F	The Princess's handmaiden
Sing Lo	F	The Princess's other handmaiden
Executioner	M	A case of losing one's head?
Surprise	M/F	Close encounters of the fourth kind
Fairy Diamante	F	The slave of the ring

NOTES
1) The Executioner and the Genie can be played by the same actor.
2) Surprise could be played by a young (small) actor dressed to represent an alien, perhaps with "tumble dryer" pipes to create long "bendy" arms.

Props

For a full list of props, see pages 126–128.

Scenaria

ACT ONE

Scene One   Outside the Emperor's courtyard, Peking

Scene Two   Still outside the Emperor's courtyard

Scene Three Widow Twanky's laundry

Scene Four   Behind the Twanky laundry

Scene Five   On Khyber Pass

INTERVAL

ACT TWO

Scene Six   Outside the Twanky laundry

Scene Seven Inside Aladdin's palace

Scene Eight Outside the Twanky laundry

Scene Nine   In the Sea of Tranquillity

Scene Ten   Community song and walkdown

FINALE

ACT
ONE

Scene One

Outside the Emperor's Courtyard - Peking.

Scenery is set with walling and trees behind large ornamental gates. On stage are stall fronts with Chinese versions of supermarket names (Tess Koh, Sanesbelly) set as a bazaar with **chorus** *as Chinese villagers. The* **Emperor** *is having a money raising fete.*

Curtains open on bustling scene and production **chorus** *number:*

SONG
"CHINATOWN"

Tableau.

Executioner *enters*

Executioner Make way, make way for the Emperor and Empress of China.

> **Chorus** *scatter.* **Emperor** *and* **Empress** *enter.* **All chorus** *bow low with hands flat together. (This bowing to the royalty occurs all through.)*

> **Emperor** *and* **Empress** *move down to the front, the* **Empress** *pulls the* **Emperor** *back so she gets there first. She addresses the audience in a haughty manner, which again is maintained throughout as she belittles the* **Emperor.**

Empress Good evening! *(cups hand to ear for reply)*

14

Audience *(little response)*

Empress *(pulling herself up to full height, sniffs)* GOOD EVENING!!

Audience GOOD EVENING!!

Empress Ah. There is someone here after all. Good. And they said they hadn't sold any tickets. There must be a secret tunnel somewhere. I wish to introduce my husband, the Emperor Ying Tong Ying Tong Ying Tong...

Chorus YIDDLE I POH!

Emperor *and* **Empress** *both look* round *disapprovingly*

Empress Emperor Ying Tong is going to say a few words.

She pauses for the **Emperor,** *but he appears to be dozing so she nudges him. He awakes with a start*

Emperor Who? What? When? Oh, is it time for bed, my little petal?

Empress *(roars loudly)* No, of course not. And don't call me that in public.

Emperor Of course not my little pet..., er sorry... darling!

Empress Oh, pull yourself together. *(He does. She walks away)*

Oh dear, I do worry for China when there are people like him in places of authority. *(turns)* You are just going to say a few words.

Emperor I am?

Empress You are!

Emperor *(pauses)* OH! *(pauses again)*

Empress Well?

Emperor Yes, not bad thank you. You?

Empress Oh, you blithering idiot, say something.

Emperor Certainly, dear... er... what about, dear?

Empress *(very agitated)* About our fete.

Emperor Fete ? What fete?

Empress Oh, for heaven's sake.

Emperor I've remembered!

Empress He always remembers right at the end. Go on then!

  Chorus *lean forward to listen.*

Emperor Oh dear, I've forgotten again.

  All groan. **Empress** *pushes him to corner of stage for confidential whisper.*

Emperor Steady on, mind the outfit, we've to take it back on Monday.

Empress Look, just for once try to act like an Emperor.

Emperor *(delighted)* Can I? Gosh, thanks.

Empress We've got to raise some money. The bills are piling up again! We're skinny.

Emperor Skinny?

Empress That's rhyming slang. Skinny lint... skint.

Emperor That's clever. I can do that. I want to Almond.

Empress Almond?

Emperor Yes, almond tart...

Empress DON'T YOU DARE!!

Emperor *(loudly)* By the way, which idiot has painted my bicycle bright yellow?

> **Executioner** *steps forward with axe over his shoulder peering down at little **Emperor**.*

Executioner I did!

> *He puts his hands together and bows. Axe nearly hits* **Emperor**.

Emperor *(gazes up in trepidation, trembling)* Oh! I just thought you'd like to know that the first coat is dry.

Empress Oh, you get worse!! Roll up, roll up, the fete is open. All sorts of goodies to buy. Roll up, roll up.

Emperor *(mimicking)* Roll up, roll up, the gate is open. All sorts of butties to buy. Roll up, roll up.

> **Empress** *signals to Executioner who hits the gong.*

SONG
"COME TO THE SUPERMARKET IN OLD PEKING"

Emperor Now, ladies and gentlemen, your attention please. This is your one and only chance to get the bargain of the year! Even [David Dickinson] can't beat this! The answer to all your problems. From Arthritis to Arf a shandy, water on the knee, a tap on the head, boils on your behind... *(all cast and* **chorus** *lose interest and start to exit as* **Emperor** *continues)* ...fallen arches, droopy drawers, headaches, heartburn and associated discomforts, athlete's foot, elephant's foot and various other miscellaneous disorders. And it's not *(two drumbeats)* one pound...

By now stage is empty. **Empress** *walks over to* **Emperor** *and taps him on the shoulder. He carries on.*

Emperor It's not *(two drumbeats)* five pounds... *(***Empress** *taps him again)* It's not even... *(two drumbeats)* twenty pounds!!

Empress I shouldn't bother!

Emperor Shush! I'm just getting into my stride.

Empress I think you've gone too far already.

Emperor *(looks round at empty stage)* Well, that's charming!!

Empress Charming! It's a disaster! You're a miracle worker.

Emperor Thanks.

Empress If you do anything that works, it's a miracle! I think I may have the answer to all our problems.

Emperor Oh, you're a wonderful woman. *(to audience)* She's a wonderful woman.

Empress You've got to persuade the Grand Vizir that his son, Prince Pekoe, would be a wonderful husband for our daughter, Lotus Blossom. They have pots of money. Come along, we've got some planning to do.

They exit. **Prince Pekoe** *and the* **Grand Vizir** *enter.*

Pekoe I don't think it's a very good idea, Father.

Vizir I can't see why not. It's the obvious solution. Look, I'll explain again. *(looks around to make sure no-one is listening)* We've fallen on hard times.

Pekoe Yes.

Vizir We need to improve our standard of living.

Pekoe Yes.

Vizir We need some extra cash.

Pekoe Yes.

Vizir So you're going to marry Princess Lotus Blossom.

Pekoe Yes.

Vizir Good.

Pekoe *(reacts)* No!!

Vizir What do you mean NO!!

Pekoe I do not want to marry the Princess.

Vizir *(to audience, smiling)* He doesn't want to marry the Princess. *(chuckles, then reacts)* YOU DON'T WANT TO

MARRY THE PRINCESS? How many men would give their right arm to marry the Princess?

Pekoe How many men would give their right arm to be ambidextrous? *(Vizir is confused)* I don't want to marry the Princess. I don't love her.

Vizir A triviality.

Pekoe It may be a triviality to you, Father, but it's very important to me.

Vizir You don't realise the position I find myself in. I am the Grand Vizir, a very eminent member of the Chinese nobility. And you – my son – Prince Pekoe, my heir.

Pekoe Your what?

Vizir My heir.

Pekoe What's the matter with your hair.

Vizir *(impatiently)* My heir, not my hair. You will eventually take up my title and position in Chinese nobility.

Pekoe Will I be able to stay in the Vizir country residence - Chinese Chequers? *(laughs)*

Vizir You are not taking this seriously. You would inherit my estate on my death.

Pekoe Well, by the sound of it there's not going to be anything to inherit. Anyway, I have promised my heart to another.

Vizir Who, in heaven's name?

Pekoe That's MY secret.

Vizir You're a big help. You might have to think about getting...
...a job.

Pekoe Oh, no! Not that!

Vizir A trip to Job Centre Plus could be the answer. *(puts an arm around* **Pekoe's** *shoulder and leads him off)* Now, what were you saying about Princess Lotus Blossom?

Pekoe exits first, **Vizir** *gives a wink to audience and exits.*

After a second or two a siren noise is heard over PA. Gets louder. Blue flashing light is seen flashing in the wings and **Wishee Washee** *bursts onto the stage on a scooter, blowing a whistle, dragging a short hosepipe behind him.*

Wishee Where's the fire, where's the fire? *(looks around disappointed)* Oh, that's a shame, someone's put it out already. I only had a ladder in my hose when I set off!! Hello, everybody. *(audience response, repeats louder)* Hello, everybody! *(better audience response)* That's better. I'm Wishee Washee and I'm the new trainee fireman. I've been doing this for three months and I've left everything in embers – November, December. Embers, get it? Oh, never mind!! *(squirts water pistol at pretend fire, then at audience)* Hey, this is fun, this is. I can see a glint in your eye, take that! We'll have none of that in here! And don't think you're going to miss out *(squirts into wings)* Hey up, I smell smoke. Could be Mum's cooking again, I'd better go, but before I do will you do something for me?

Audience *(little response)*

Wishee *(pause with hands on hips)* Thank you for that huge and immediate response! Come on, you've paid your money, so you may as well enjoy yourselves. Let's try again. Will you do something for me?

Audience Yes!!

Wishee Lovely!! Each time I come on stage I'll shout, "Hello, folks" and I want you to shout, "Hello, Wishee". Will you do that? *(moves across stage)* WILL YOU DO THAT?

Audience YES!!

Wishee Fantastic. This may come as a total surprise to you but we're going to have a practice. Are you ready? Well, what was that? I said ARE YOU READY?

Audience YES.

Wishee That's better. Here goes. *(exits and returns)* HELLO, FOLKS!

Audience HELLO, WISHEE.

Wishee *(moves across stage)* LOUDER ... HELLO, FOLKS.

Audience HELLO, WISHEE.

Wishee OGGIE, OGGIE, OGGIE,!

Audience Oy, Oy, Oy,!

Wishee OGGIE

Audience Oy!

Wishee OGGIE

Audience Oy!

Wishee OGGIE, OGGIE, OGGIE,!

Audience Oy, Oy, Oy,!

Wishee OOMPAH , OOMPAH

Audience STICK IT UP YOUR JUMPER!

Wishee That's brilliant, fantastic, absolutely wonderful - and you weren't bad either. See you later. Bye!!

>**Wishee** *exits waving. Siren starts up again and fades out into distance.*

Widow Twanky *(offstage)* Aladdin! Aladdin! Oh, where is that idle laundry boy son of mine! *(enters)* Aladdin! ALADDIN!!

She walks across stage, stops abruptly and sees audience.

Oh! Hello. *(peers at them)* I didn't think there were so many people in Peking! You don't look very Chinese to me either. Oh, well, never mind. Aladdin! Aladdin!! Where are you? Kids! I don't know what to do with them. There's Aladdin, *(aside)* he's my eldest, a right lazy scoundrel. Never there when you want him. Then there's Wishee Washee, *(aside)* he's my youngest. He's so full of energy he just never stops. Never stops ripping the laundry, flooding the place, getting the colours mixed up with the whites. I don't know. I wish I'd stayed a Virgo instead of becoming a Sagittarian. Life would have been a lot quieter. Mind you, we've had a hard life.

(pauses looking sad to collect Aaaahs from the audience) Yes ... I lost me husband. *(Aaaaah)* Yes, I sent him to the shop for some peas and I haven't seen him since. I was frantic, I didn't know WHAT to do – then I remembered I'd got some beans in the cupboard!! When Aladdin and Wishee Washee were little, we were so poor, one of them was made in Hong Kong... When they were born we couldn't afford the stork, they came by second class post... We were that poor, even the rainbows round our street were in black and white.

Never mind. That's all in the past. We've got the laundry now. That gives us a living. That's when we can get some washing done, that is. *(looks off one side)* Aladdin! *(goes to other side)* Aladdin! Oh, dear. Where can he be? You haven't seen Aladdin, have you?

Audience No!!

Twanky Well, have you seen Wishee Washee then?

Audience Yes!!

Twanky You have? Which way did he go?

Audience That way!

Twanky Oh, I bet he's still trying to put fires out, isn't he? That's his latest craze but it's getting past a joke. Get it ? PASTA JOKE? *(laughs, gives up, talks into wings confidentially)* It's going to be an early finish tonight, get the burgers on! *(back to audience)* He's put out the boiler in the laundry three times this week so far. Anyway, I've got to find Aladdin, so will you help me?

Audience YES!!

Twanky Come on, you'll have to shout louder than that. Will you help me?

Audience YES!!

Twanky Gosh, that's fantastic. You're all hired for crowd duty at [the Shay] on Saturday. What I want you to do is to shout for Aladdin with me. Will you do that?

Audience YES!!

Twanky Brilliant, after three. One… two… THREE.

Audience ALADDIN!!

Twanky *(looks around)* No! He mustn't have heard us. Try again and louder this time. One… two… THREE.

Audience ALADDIN!!

Aladdin *wanders in at the back, stretching and yawning. He has clothes draped on him, including a bra.*

Aladdin *(yawns)* Ah – ah. Hello mum. Did you call?

Twanky Did I call? Did I call? There were *(turns and looks)* twenty-five of us shouting our blinking heads off, weren't we?

Audience YES!

Twanky And just look at you. *(pulling clothes off him)* You've been sleeping in the laundry basket again, haven't you? *(takes bra off him and holds it up)* Either that or you're turning into a travesty.

Aladdin Oh no, not a chance. Cross my heart. *(glance at audience)* Anyway, I've only been here a few minutes.

Twanky I don't know. You'd sleep all night and you'd sleep all day if you had the chance.

SONG
"LAZY BONES"

End of song. **Twanky** *and* **Aladdin** *start to exit at opposite sides.* **Twanky** *notices and grabs* **Aladdin** *by ear and drags him off to laundry.*

Sinister vaudeville music, after a few bars of which **Abanazer** *enters. Then* **Wishee Washee** *enters at other side.* **Abanazer** *is wearing sheikh style costume – flowing robes and head covered.*

Wishee HELLO, FOLKS.

Audience HELLO, WISHEE.

Wishee Super. Fabulous. Oooh, I could crush a grape! *(spots* **Abanazer***)* Ey up. He looks a bit strange, doesn't he? He looks like he got up in a bit of a hurry and brought his bedclothes with him. He looks a bit of a rogue as well.

Abanazer *comes over and puts his hand on* **Wishee's** *shoulder on next lines.*

I think I ought to run back to the laundry and warn my mother and Aladdin that... *(speech slows down as he realises)* ...there's someone strange... *(looks at* **Abanazer***)* ...in the neighbourhood and things don't... *(looks at*

Abanazer, *speech speeds up)*...seem altogether right and I'm starting to get a bit nervous and I think I want to go home.

Wishee *turns and tries to go and* **Abanazer** *stops him running off.*

Abanazer Hello, effendi.

Wishee Effendi? Effendi? That's not very nice. You're not from [Halifax], are you?

Abanazer No. Effendi means friend in Arabic. I come from Arabia.

Wishee I bet that took you a long time. I say, you're not the Sheikh of Araby are you?

Abanazer No.

Wishee You're not a Milk Sheikh by any chance?

Abanazer NO!! I'm an Oil Sheikh.

Wishee An Oil Sheikh. *(whistles) (aside)* I bet this fellow's loaded with money.

Abanazer *(moves to other side of stage) (aside)* That's started sowing the seeds of my plot, I bet he thinks I'm loaded with money. *(sinister laugh, pulling boos from audience, moves back to centre stage)*

Wishee You can answer a question for me Alfonso!

Abanazer Effendi. *(***Wishee** *crosses in front of* **Abanazer***)*

Wishee *(reacts as if "goosed")* Hey, watch it. Listen, you know all these petrol stations that keep springing up everywhere?

Abanazer Yes.

Wishee Well, how do they know there's petrol underneath before they build them?

Abanazer How do they know there's petrol underneath... ? You're crackers!!

Wishee Yes, Chinese crackers. No, I'm Wishee Washee. What's your name?

Abanazer *(very importantly)* I am the Great Sheikh Abanazer, a wonderful magician from the East *(aside)* and aspiring to be the richest man in the world, but more about that later. *(laughs sinisterly)*

Wishee Hey, he's full of Eastern promise.
(sings and mimes Egyptian dance)
It was in Baghdad
Where me mother met me dad
And went folly lolly doodle all the day.

Abanazer You are a fool. Are there any Chinese people with brains?

Wishee Oh, yes. Chinese people are very clever. They're all very good at multiplication.

Abanazer Oh, I give up. This fellow is not going to be able to help me with my plans. I'll try somewhere else. Good day to you. *(bows in Eastern fashion, exits)*

Wishee What a weird character. I bet he's up to no good. We'll have to keep an eye on him. Magician, is he? *(looks off stage)* Not a very good one. He's just turned into a cul-de-sac. I'm off to warn mother. See you later. Bye bye. *(exits waving)*

Curtain.

<u>End of Scene One</u>

Scene Two

Still outside **Emperor's** *courtyard. Curtains open.* **Princess** *and handmaidens are on stage.* **Princess** *has a Chinese fan.*

Sing Hi Then what will you do, Princess?

Princess I don't know what to do, Sing Hi. I know my father and mother have problems with the Royal Mint.

Sing Lo Yes, it seems to have a hole in it.

Princess You're right, Sing Lo. But I don't see why I should have to marry Prince Pekoe just to help out the finances. It's not right. I don't like him very much.

Sing Hi Oh, I do Princess.

Princess Sing Hi! I never knew!

Sing Hi Well, we've kept it a secret. It didn't seem right that a Prince should be interested in a common hand maiden. It's not fair.

Princess I know just what you mean. We'll have to do something about it. I need to spend some time on my own to think seriously about things. You two go back to the palace and I will join you later.

Sing Lo Oh, Princess, I don't think you should. If any man looks at you, they will have their head chopped off.

Princess Nonsense, Sing Lo. No-one will know who I am. Now, run along, both of you.

Sing Hi *and* **Sing Lo** *exit, unhappily.*

Princess *(to audience)* You don't know how lucky you are. Being a princess can become very tedious at times. There are so many official functions to perform; I never feel I can do what I want to do, when I want to do it. But now I've got a chance to be ordinary - at least for a little while.

SONG
"SOMEONE TO WATCH OVER ME"

At the end of the song, **Aladdin** *comes swinging in with some parcels of laundry for the palace.* **Aladdin** *sees* **Princess**, *stops abruptly, looks at* **Princess** *and audience, nods and smiles and clears his throat.*

Aladdin Hello.

Princess *(surprised)* Oh, hello.

Aladdin I was just thinking to myself, who is that lovely creature over there?

Princess Over where? *(coyly)* You mean me?

Aladdin Of course. Forgive me for saying so, but you are lovely. I want to take you away from all this.

Princess This is so sudden.

Aladdin I know, once I get going, I'm quick. They didn't know whether to call me Aladdin or Lamborghini! What's your name?

Princess I'm P... er... I'm Sing Hi, handmaiden to Princess Lotus Blossom, the Emperor's daughter.

Aladdin Oh dear, that must be boring.

Princess Why?

Aladdin Well, I've heard that the Princess is very stuck up, thoroughly miserable and obstinate.

Princess You have, have you?

Aladdin Yes. I bet looking after her is a real pain.

Princess Well, for your information, the Princess is a very nice person.

Aladdin I think you'd say that even if she wasn't.

Princess I think you'd think I'd say that even if I didn't.

Aladdin Pardon?

Princess Granted.

Aladdin Well, I think she must be a real stick in the mud, but I like you. I've got to go deliver this laundry to the palace. Hey, you could take it back with you, couldn't you? Do you mind?

Princess Well, I'm not... er, *(smiles and softens)* alright, I'll take it for you.

Aladdin Thanks, you're a cracker.

Princess I think I should go now before someone comes.

Aladdin Aw, do you have to? I was just getting to know you. Can I see you again?

Princess I don't know.

Aladdin Oh, please say yes.

Vizir *enters upstage.*

Princess Look out, the Grand Vizir is here. He mustn't see you speaking to me. Please go.

Aladdin Meet me at the laundry tomorrow.

Princess Oh, alright.

Aladdin I can't wait. Bye.

Aladdin *exits smartly.*

Princess *hides her face behind her fan.*

Vizir You there. What are you doing out here?

Princess Er... er... I'm taking some laundry back to the palace for the Princess.

Vizir Do they not deliver, these Chinese peasants. They want locking up and I may see to it myself.

Princess Oh, no, they usually deliver the laundry themselves, it's just that – er – that they had a bit of a staff problem.

Vizir The only staff problem they have are the Twankies themselves. They're the problem.

Princess I think you're mistaken Grand Vizir.

Vizir How dare you suggest I am mistaken. You are but a handmaiden in the Emperor's Palace. You had better remember your position. Now back to the palace at once.

Princess Certainly, Eminence. *(bows)* Immediately. *(bows again and exits)*

Vizir I don't know. These young girls just don't seem to know their place. They are spoilt, that's the trouble. I wonder where that son of mine is. Pekoe! *(looks about)* Pekoe! He is being a trifle difficult about his betrothal to Princess Lotus Blossom. I can't understand his reluctance. If I was ten years younger – *(looks closely at audience)* – alright, thirty years younger. Anyway, he'd better change his mind, and quickly. We need the Emperor's wealth to keep us going. We're getting flat on our uppers. Convincing Pekoe is the difficult bit. *(goes towards wings)* Pekoe!!

Vizir *exits.*

Vaudeville comedy music (Looney Tunes?) and **Chop Suey** *and* **Chow Mein** *enter with placards advertising Chinese takeaway – "Chinese Garden Takeaway".*

Chop Suey Now this is a good pitch to advertise our new takeaway. The Emperor's Palace is just over there.

Chow Mein Do you think they'll mind? I mean it doesn't seem too respectful.

Chop Suey Oh, you are a coward, aren't you? Nobody got any selling done by being respectful. You're just like your name Chow Mein, all soft and noodly. Not like me, Chop Suey.

Chow Mein *(aside)* He'll get a karate chop suey if he's not careful, right up his sarong. *(to* **Chop Suey***)* I feel a right nit with this placard.

34

Chop Suey You look a right nit anyway. Even more so with a placard.

Chow Mein *(aside)* I'll wrap it round his head in a minute He's getting right up my nose. *(to* **Chop Suey***)* I've just thought of a good name for you.

Chop Suey What's that?

Chow Mein Vick. Ha ha ha, *(turns to audience)* Vick, ha, ha ha. Do you get it, Vick, he gets right up my nose, ha ha ha... Oh, please yourself. *(He slopes his placard)*

Chop Suey Now come on, concentrate if you can. Present arms. *(He does)*

Chow Mein *tries to do same and throws placard over his shoulder.*

Chop Suey And what's that then? You'll never get in the Boys' Brigade like that.

Chow Mein Sorry, I just got excited, Tommy... er... Chop. *(picks up his placard)*

Chop Suey Look, I'll show you what to do. *(throws his placard down.* **Chow Mein** *does the same)* What did you do that for?

Chow Mein I did what you did.

Chop Suey Well, pick it up again.

Chow Mein *bends down to pick up his placard, stands up and turns with placard as if to hit* **Chop Suey***, but* **Chop Suey** *bends down to pick up his own placard.* **Chow Mein** *spins back again and this time hits* **Chop Suey** *on the* *back and he falls flat on his face. Percussion noises. **Chop Suey** pulls himself up by **Chow Mein's** costume till they are standing facing each other almost touching noses.*

Chop Suey *(spraying)* I suppose you think that's funny!

Chow Mein *wipes his eyes.*

Chow Mein I think it's starting to rain.

Chop Suey Look, take your placard and just hold it up straight so people can see it. *(shouts loudly)* CALL AT THE CHINESE GARDEN RESTAURANT, GOOD QUICK FOOD, NO MESS, NO TIME, NO WASHING UP.

Chow Mein NO SWEAT.

Chop Suey *(hitting him)* Just behave yourself. *(look into wings)* Ha ha! Our first customer!

Abanazer *enters from the wings.*

Abanazer Good day, gentlemen. I am the Great Abanazer.

Chop Suey And I am Chop Suey, part owner of the Chinese Garden Take Away, and this is the other part, Chow Mein. Would you like to partake of our delicious recipes? *(looks proudly and winks at **Chow Mein**)*

Abanazer What?! I am an Arab!

Chow Mein Hard luck.

Abanazer How dare you! You dregs of Chinatown!

Chop Suey Now, look here, Mr Ebenezer.

Abanazer ABANAZER.

Chop Suey That too! There's no need to get excited.

Abanazer I am the Greatest Magician in the world. Do not meddle with me.

Chow Mein I wouldn't dream of it. *(steps aside)* I'm not like that.

Chop Suey Come on, Chow Mein. I think this situation calls for some old Chinese courage and fortitude.

Chow Mein I think you're right. Let's go for a pint.

> **Chop Suey** and **Chow Mein** *exit pronto to wind whistle - cartoon exit.*

Abanazer Is this whole country full of idiotic Chinamen. So far, I haven't found anyone who can help me in my scheme. *(looks around in a sinister way with much flapping of cape)* I am not in this forsaken place because I like China - or its people. Nay, my intentions are much more profitable. *(laughs and wrings his hands)* By fair means or foul, and you can guess which, ha ha ha, I have come into possession of Ancient Writings which tell of a vast treasure hidden in a magic cave not far from here. *(dramatically)* BUT!... *(looks around)* ...more important than the vast fortune of jewels... ...there is a lamp, a magic lamp which will make me the ruler of the Universe. More important than [Boris Johnson], even more important than [Jean-Claude Juncker]. Well, nearly anyway. But I need the services of a righteous young man; only one such young person can enter the jewelled cave. So far, everyone I've met has been an idiot. There must be someone in China who's got some sense.

Widow Twanky *enters.* **Abanazer** *is deep in thought.*

Twanky *(sees* **Abanazer***, pulls up and steps back admiringly)* Oooh, for a minute I thought it was porridge – no that's wrong, a pottage, no, a menage – no – a mirage, that's it, a mirage. Just looks like an oasis in the desert – well, you know what I mean. Just look at him, a fine figure of a man. You can see from the lines on his face – and there's plenty of lines on his face – you can tell this is a solid, honest, reliable, upstanding member of the Eastern community. *(***Abanazer** *laughs silently at audience)* Don't you think so boys and girls?

Audience NO!!

Twanky Oh, yes he is. *(***Abanazer** *nods silently)*

Audience Oh, no he isn't.

Twanky *(and* **Abanazer** *miming and nodding)* Oh, yes he is!!

Audience OH, NO HE ISN'T!

Abanazer }
Twanky   } OH, YES HE IS!! *(shouting loudly)*

Audience Oh, no he isn't!

Abanazer *(waves arms menacingly)* SILENCE!!
(in rhyme)
You scum of the earth, you ignorant rabble,
No more of this ranting and low-minded twaddle.

Bow down with respect in my company,
Or some of you perish, maybe one, two or three!
(Widow Twanky *is becoming rather scared and nervous)*
Big monsters will come and will frighten you all.
Big beasties so hungry, they'll eat up the small,
And then start with the big ones like you over there…

Twanky Let them start with that lady, I don't like her hair…
Oh, I'm sorry what am I saying.

Abanazer Oh, pardon me, dear lady. *(bows low)*

Twanky Oh! I say, you can beg my pardon any time. *(She curtsies clumsily)*

Abanazer *(He catches her)* Now, steady on, my dear. *(She wobbles trying to stand up)*

Twanky Oh, this is it! My wildest dreams have come true. A sheikh about to whisk me away on his horse across the desert into the moonlight to join his… his…

Abanazer Harem?

Twanky No, I can't hear 'em, I'm dreaming. Well, are you ready? Where's yer 'orse?

Abanazer I haven't got a 'orse.

Twanky Oh, flipping heck. Wouldn't you know it. First time I get to meet a sheikh and he doesn't know the story. Have you not seen Omar Sharif?

Abanazer No, but I've seen Old Mother Riley. But hist… hist… *(pauses)*

Twanky Hist? What's hist?

Abanazer Listen.

Twanky I'm listening, I'm listening.

Abanazer I have been sent by my country on a secret mission.

Twanky *(impressed)* Oooh! Top secret?

Abanazer Absolutely!

Twanky Classified?

Abanazer Yes, if you're not careful. Now, I need an assistant!

Twanky *(excited)* Yes!

Abanazer One whom I can trust.

Twanky Oh, yes!

Abanazer One who is virtuous and righteous.

Twanky *(thinks)* Will just righteous do?

Abanazer A young man as well.

Twanky Oh, dash!

Abanazer There's money in it!

Twanky *(eyes light up)* MONEY? How much?

Abanazer More than you've ever seen.

Twanky *(to audience)* I knew he was rich. When you get to my age you get a nose for these things. Hey, watch it you!

Abanazer I don't suppose you know of a virtuous, righteous young man who would help?

Twanky When does he get paid?

Abanazer As soon as the work is done.

Twanky It's not dangerous is it?

Abanazer Of course not.

Twanky Oh, that's alright then. Well, I have two boys, Aladdin and Wishee Washee.

Abanazer Not Wishee Washee! I've met him already. I don't think he will do. But Aladdin I would like to meet.

Twanky Well, come round to the laundry tomorrow. He'll be there.

Abanazer I shall be there, dear lady. Don't forget. *(puts his fingers to his lips and departs.* **Twanky** *puts her fingers to her lips and stands arms outstretched in mock swoon)*

Twanky *(unfreezes with a start)* Oooh! Isn't it exciting, espionage, cloaks and daggers, snakes and ladders, and pots of money. What couldn't I do to a pot of money. I could get a new outfit and have my face lifted. I could have my initials in gold on the bags under my eyes. Oh, *(sighs)* isn't it wonderful to be rich. *(starts to exit with her head in the air, stops)* Riff raff. *(She exits)*

Curtain closes. Scene changes to laundry.

Enter **Emperor**, **Empress**, **Vizir** *and* **Executioner** *in front of tabs.*

Empress Now, come along Ying Tong. Now's the time for a proclamation about the betrothal of our daughter to Prince Pekoe.

Vizir Hear, hear. Let's put the record straight.

Emperor But, my dear, Lotus Blossom does not seem to be too keen on the idea.

Empress Now, Ying Tong, you know very well that people in our circles can't always do what they want to.

Vizir Hear, hear.

They look at him.

Empress Just think how many times marriages take place between royal families to bring strength and riches together.

Vizir Hear, hear.

They glare at him.

Emperor Well, if you're sure my dear.

Empress I'm sure.

Vizir Hear, hear!

Emperor, Empress and Executioner OH BE QUIET!!

Executioner Honestly, where do they get these actors from these days?

Empress Right, Executioner. Have you got the proclamation?

Executioner Right here your Majesty. *(takes out scroll)*

Empress Right, we will announce this proclamation in the traditional way. Are you ready?

Emperor Ready.

Vizir Ready.

Executioner Ready.

Empress Right.

They all sing Ying Tong song first line.

Empress Stop, stop!!

Emperor What's the matter?

Empress Someone is a rotten singer.

Emperor Well, it's not me.

Vizir It's not me.

Executioner Don't look at me.

Empress Very well. *(takes gun out of her pocket)* Left turn. Left, right, left, right, etc.

They march into wings. A shot is heard. **Empress,** **Emperor** *and* **Executioner** *return* **Emperor** *notices* **Vizir** *is missing.*

Empress Right then, let's have another try.

They sing first line again.

Empress Someone is a terrible singer.

Emperor Well, it isn't me.

Executioner And it's not me.

Empress Very well. Left turn.

They march off into wings, a shot is heard. **Empress** *and* **Emperor***, looking decidedly nervous, come back on.*

Empress Now then, are you ready?

Emperor Can I make a last request?

Empress No! Ready?

They sing line again. **Emperor** *turns left and slowly walks off without instructions,* **Empress** *follows beaming. A shot is heard.* **Emperor** *comes back on.*

Emperor Someone's a rotten shot.

Musical Director Yes, but I'm not.

Musical Director *fires a shot.* **Emperor** *lifts his costume to reveal pants round his ankles. Blackout.*

End of Scene Two

Scene Three

Still in front of tabs. Enter **Chop Suey** *and* **Chow Mein**.

Chop Suey This is awful.

Chow Mein I know.

Chop Suey You know what we are now, don't you? We are the Emperor's hired henchmen.

Chow Mein And what about the proclamation? Now the Princess is betrothed to Prince Pekoe, any man who looks at the Princess is going to have his head chopped off. So how can we follow the Princess with our eyes shut?

Chop Suey Why with your eyes shut?

Chow Mein I don't want my head to be chopped off.

Chop Suey *(hits him)* You idiot, he doesn't mean us, he means anyone else.

Chow Mein *(positively)* NO, I won't do it!! *(folds his arms.)*

Chop Suey Why not for heaven's sake?

Chow Mein It's not fair.

Chop Suey *(gets out money pouch and shakes it)* This might help you change your mind.

Chow Mein No!

Chop Suey We've been paid in advance.

Chow Mein NO!

Chop Suey Quite a lot of money.

Chow Mein NO! Absolutely, definitely, positively, NOT!! *(moves to* **Chop Suey***)* How much?

Chop Suey Twenty gold pieces – each!

Chow Mein *(almost drooling, looking at bag, hesitating Hamlet tune plays)* Alright.

Chop Suey Good. Right. I think we could maybe do with a disguise.

Chow Mein Good idea – I'll go as Spiderman!

Chop Suey Give me strength!! *(clouts him)* Come on, I'll make a sleuth out of you yet.

Chow Mein What's a sleuth?

Chop Suey Oh, never mind. Come on.

Curtains open.

Laundry scene.

Busily active as music plays "WHISTLE WHILE YOU WORK"

Widow Twanky, **Aladdin** *and* **Wishee Washee** *are in production line washing situation to the music.* **Some dancers (chorus** *helping if necessary) rinsing in one tub, washing in another, pretend drying in another, folding up, putting in a bag. Noises like scrubbing board, bell, whistles, wind whistle to music. Comedy ending.*

Wishee HELLO, FOLKS

Audience HELLO, WISHEE

Twanky Phew, it's a long time since we were so busy. Everyone must be sending their smalls at the same time.

Wishee Not all of them are smalls. *(holds up large bloomers)*

Aladdin I bet they belong to the Empress. (**Wishee** *and* **Aladdin** *are in hysterics)*

Twanky You mustn't laugh at things like that. It's not nice. Besides... they're mine.

> **Wishee** *and* **Aladdin** *laugh even louder.* **Twanky** *snatches them and tucks them up her own bloomers.*

Twanky *(to audience)* I know this is a bit snobbish, but I do have more than one pair.

Aladdin I have eight sets of underclothes.

Wishee Why eight?

Aladdin Well, Monday, Tuesday, Wednesday, Thursday, Friday, Saturday, Sunday and one spare.

Twanky Hee hee, hark at you. I'll have you know I have twelve sets.

Wishee That's right. January, February, March...

Twanky HOW DARE YOU? Come on, get back to work. We've got all these to do yet.

Aladdin Oh, Crikey!

Twanky What on earth is the matter?

Aladdin The Emperor's long johns are in the starch.

Wishee I always thought he was a big stiff!

> **Aladdin** *brings out cardboard cut-out of long johns and brings them to front.*

Twanky *(flapping)* Oh, what are we going to do? We can't take them back like this! We'll all be beheaded! Oh, help!

Aladdin Now, calm down Mother. I don't think it's a capital offence. *(puts cut-out away)*

Twanky I'm not so sure about that! You heard the proclamation. He's going to chop off the head of any man who looks at the Princess. Can you imagine what he'll do when he finds out what's happened to his long johns. Oh, what can we do?

Wishee I know what we can do.

Twanky What's that?

Wishee Let's put our faith in the patron saint of Chinese launderers.

Twanky Who's that?

Wishee Why, it's Mr Wu, of course.

SONG
"MR WU"

Aladdin, Wishee, Twanky, chorus, dancers

After song, **chorus** *and* **dancers** *exit*

Twanky Aren't they a lovely audience?

Wishee Yes – intelligent too. Half of them are leaving.

Aladdin Now, do you feel better?

Twanky Not a lot. But we won't tell him till tomorrow.

Aladdin Now, Mother. You mustn't procrastinate.

Twanky *(wide eyed)* I never…

Aladdin You shouldn't put off till tomorrow what you can do today.

Wishee *(quickly)* 'Cos if you do it today and like it, you can do it again tomorrow.

Twanky Oh, you do get me confused at times. Come along. We'd better get on with this lot.

They restart getting ready for washing. Knocking noise. **Twanky** *goes to the door.*

Twanky Oooh – some more customers. Word is getting round about our service.

Aladdin I hope not.

Twanky *exits and comes back on with* **Sing Hi** *and* **Sing Lo***.*

Twanky And what can Twanky's laundry do for you two girls? Where are your clothes?

Sing Lo Why, we've got them on!

Twanky Well, this is a little unusual.

Wishee But it's not a bad idea.

Sing Lo Can you help us?

Wishee No problem!

Aladdin We don't have a changing room!

Sing Hi We don't need one. We'll stay here.

> **Aladdin** and **Wishee** do high fives.

Twanky Oh, give up you two. I don't know if I can cope with this. These modern times are going to have a lot to answer for. Oh well. You can't be a stick in the mud for ever. Come on, take them off.

Sing Lo Pardon?

Aladdin }
Wishee } She said take them off. *(expectant smiles)*

Sing Hi Take what off?

Twanky Your clothes.

> **Sing Hi** and **Sing Lo** *giggle and hide their faces with their fans in embarrassment.*

Twanky Look, if it makes you feel better, I'll join you.

> *"Stripper" music starts and* **Twanky** *starts undressing to reveal bloomers/corset etc. show style.*

Sing Hi *(moves to* **Twanky** *and taps her on shoulder)* I don't think you understand. We haven't come for clothes washing, we've come to see Aladdin.

Twanky *(in sudden shock)* You mean you don't want – you're not going to – *(***Sing Hi** *and* **Sing Lo** *keep shaking their heads)* – Well, why didn't you say – HELP!! *(She exits fast)*

Aladdin Sorry about the confusion. She usually gets the wrong end of the stick.

Wishee And we usually get the other end.

Aladdin I'm Aladdin, what can I do for you?

Sing Hi This is Sing Lo and I am Sing Hi.

Aladdin No, you're not.

Sing Hi Yes, I am!

Aladdin *(to* **Wishee***)* Oh, no she's not.

Sing Hi *(encourages audience)* Oh, yes she is.

Aladdin OH NO, SHE ISN'T.

Sing Hi   }
Sing Lo   } OH YES, SHE IS.
Audience }

Aladdin I met Sing Hi yesterday – and that wasn't you.

Sing Hi The girl you met yesterday was not Sing Hi, that was the Princess.

Aladdin The Princess?

Wishee The proclamation.

Aladdin The Emperor?

Wishee The Executioner.

Sing Lo And the Princess is on her way here to see you, as you arranged.

Aladdin That's marvellous. You should see her. So beautiful, so refined, so – interesting.

Sing Lo I go see if they are near and make sure there are no guards about.

Sing Lo *exits.*

Aladdin Hear that, Wishee? She is a real-life princess. Oh no!

Wishee What's the matter?

Aladdin I think I said some unkind things about the Princess. She told me she was one of the Princess's handmaidens. I hope she didn't take offence!

Wishee It doesn't seem like it if she's coming to see you today. I don't know how you do it. You have a habit of falling on your feet.

Knocks heard at side. **Wishee** *goes to door.*

Enter **Princess, Pekoe, Sing Lo** *and* **Wishee**.

Sing Hi Oh, Pekoe. *(She goes to him)*

Pekoe Hello, Sing Hi, we can have another few moments together.

Aladdin *moves to* **Princess.**

Aladdin Hello again. I haven't thought about anyone or anything else but you since yesterday.

Wishee *bursts into a fit of coughing.*
Aladdin *glares at* **Wishee.**

Aladdin By the way Princess...

Princess Oh, you know?

Aladdin Yes, and I am sorry that I said what I did yesterday. I know now that I was mistaken.

Princess That is very nice of you.

Pekoe *and* **Sing Hi, Aladdin** *and* **Princess** *continue silent chatting.* **Wishee Washee** *moves nervously over to* **Sing Lo.**

Wishee I don't see why we should get left out of all this, do you?

Sing Lo I certainly do not. Hello, I'm Sing Lo.

Wishee I'm Wishee Washee. I don't suppose you're looking for a husband, by any chance?

Sing Lo The man that I marry will be as noble as Ho Chi Min, as brave as Hercules, as wise as Solomon and as handsome as Justin Bieber.

Wishee How fortunate that we met.

Aladdin *(to* **Princess***)* Can I meet you later?

Princess I'm not sure about that, you're nearly a perfect stranger.

Aladdin Who's perfect?

Knocks at the door, **Wishee Washee** *goes and comes back with* **Chow Mein** *and* **Chop Suey** *looking suspicious in black cloaks and hats. As they come in* **Twanky** *comes back on and sees the newcomers.*

Twanky Good heavens, it's getting quite full in here. *(sees* **Chop** *and* **Chow***)* Oh, I see you changed your minds.

Chop Suey What?

Twanky You've taken you clothes off!

Chow Mein What kind of place is this?

Chop Suey *(looks around)* Come along, I think we've seen enough. We have our duty to perform.

Chow Mein Do we have to? Looks like fun here.

Chop Suey Of course we have. We have to uphold the Chinese royal proclamation. *(exits)*

Chow Mein *(reluctantly)* We have – sniff – to uphold – sniff – the Chinese – sniff – royal proclamation – *(bursts into tears and exits)*

Twanky What weird people - why can't they all be normal like us? You know those two look like the owners of the Chinese Garden Takeaway. They're a right pair of dummies. I complained that a chicken I'd bought was rubbery. He just said, "Tank you velly much".

Pekoe I think it is too risky for us all to be together in here. Besides, we are holding up the laundry.

Twanky Oh, don't worry about that. It normally works this fast.

Pekoe Even so, we must all be very careful. We now have this unfortunate proclamation, and similar problems with my father, the Grand Vizir.

Princess Yes, they are obsessed by the idea of Prince Pekoe and I marrying each other, for all the wrong reasons.

Pekoe And we both wish to be free to find our own partners, but it is very difficult.

Aladdin Yes, parents can be difficult at times.

Twanky Just watch it you. *(all laugh)* Well, enjoy our time together while you can. Come on out the back way, then you won't be seen. But you'll have to stay here, Wishee.

Wishee Aw! That's not fair.

Sing Lo Don't worry. I'll see you again if you want to!

Wishee Oooh, yes please.

Twanky Come along then.

> **Princess, Aladdin, Pekoe, Sing Hi** *and* **Sing Lo** *exit.*

Twanky Now come on, Wishee, we've just got this load to do for them posh folk up at [Skircoat Green] and then we've done.

Wishee *gets hold of bucket near one of tubs, swills it round and splashes* **Twanky**.

Twanky Hey, watch out, you splashed me then. *(wipes her face)*

Wishee I'm sorry, I didn't mean to. I was just making sure this was properly mixed up, like this. *(splashes her again. She wipes her face)*

Twanky That's twice now, you take that. *(dips her hand in bucket and flicks it at* **Wishee***)*

Wishee *(wipes his face)* That's not fair, I got more than you did. *(flicks some back)*

Twanky Right, just you wait. *(scoops lather (shaving cream) into a hat/cap like a bowler with a hole in the top and advances on* **Wishee***)*

Wishee What have you got there? Now, now.

They circle round a bit, **Twanky** *distracts his attention by pointing off stage and slaps hat on* **Wishee's** *head. Cream shoots up out of hole in middle of hat.* **Wishee** *takes off hat and wipes his face.* **Twanky** *is in hysterics.*

Wishee That's done it. You've had it now. *(He picks up a bucket and moves towards* **Twanky***.* **Twanky** *picks up another bucket as she passes round)*

Twanky Now, just calm down, enough is enough, we've got to get this washing done. It's not going to do itself you know.

Wishee I'll do it as soon as I've emptied this bucket.

They are now circling faster, then they stop, one at each side of rear corner entrance. They face up to each other.

Twanky OK, then. Go for your gun.

Wishee When I can see the whites of your eyes.

Twanky You'll have a long wait then.

Wishee One.

Twanky One.

Wishee Two.

Twanky Two.

Chop Suey *(from offstage loudly)* Here they are your majesties!

> **Emperor** *and* **Empress** *dash in quickly between* **Wishee** *and* **Twanky***.*

Wishee }
Twanky } THREE

> *They cover* **Emperor** *and* **Empress** *in goo.*

Twanky *(to* **Wishee***)* Now look what you've done. What are we going to do now?

Wishee RUN?

Empress What on earth do you think you're doing. Hooligans, idiots!!

> **Twanky** *rushes for towels and starts wiping them down. They snatch towels.* **Twanky** *gets down on her knees.*

Twanky Oh a thousand – nay a MILLION apologies, your Highness.

Wishee And a couple from me too.

Emperor This is no way to treat your rulers. You will be beheaded. That reminds me... *(looks around)* So, we've been brought on a fool's errand. Where is the Princess?

Chop Suey They were here your Highness.

Aladdin *comes in from the other side.*

Aladdin What's all the commotion about? CRIKEY, what have you done?

Chop Suey }
Chow Mein } THAT'S HIM!

Empress So, you're the one who has defied the Emperor's proclamation. Seize him!

Chop Suey *and* **Chow Mein** *grab* **Aladdin**.

Empress Call for the Executioner.

Shouts of "Call the executioner" ring out along backstage.

Aladdin You may behead me if you like, for the love of your daughter, but don't think such a stupid proclamation can last for long.

Empress Such impudence! Silence yourself, you Chinese serf. Where is the Executioner?

Executioner enters with axe, **Grand Vizir** follows.

Vizir Here he is your majesties! Prepare the prisoner!

Aladdin *is forced to the ground in front of basket.*

Twanky Oh, don't chop his head off, he'll have nowhere to put his cap!! Please save him. I'll do anything!

Emperor Anything?

Empress Ying Tong! Behave!

Emperor Sorry, my dear.

Aladdin Mother, if I get any mail, put it in the basket, I'll read it later.

Twanky *starts crying.*

Grand Vizir Get ready, executioner! *(drum roll)*

Executioner *steps forward, slowly lifts axe above his head – ratchet sound.*

Vizir Ready! One… *(gasps from the crowd)*

Vizir Two… *(gasps from crowd.* **Abanazer** *rushes on stage, assumes suitable posture)*

Abanazer STOP!

Drum roll stops. Everyone freezes. Ominous roll on timpani.

With all the strength of my magical powers

 I control the destiny of all around,

From beneath the ground to the top of the towers

There'll be no movement, there'll be no sound

Unless I decree it by way of favour

No-one else this soul can save.

Now perhaps my plan and Aladdin's labours

Will get me to the magic cave.

Abanazer *goes to* **Aladdin** *and clicks him awake.*

Aladdin What's happening? Who are you? *(sees* **Executioner***)* Yikes! *(jumps out of way)* What's the matter with everyone?

Abanazer They are under my spell. I have saved your life. Permit me to introduce myself. I am the Great Abanazer, Sheikh and magician. You may call me Uncle Abanazer.

Aladdin Well, Uncle Banana, I'm really grateful to you.

Abanazer My name is A-BA-NA-ZER.

Aladdin I'll try to remember. Can you wake my Mother and Wishee Washee?

Abanazer *snaps* **Wishee** *and* **Twanky***.*

Abanazer Now, Aladdin, I want you to come with me. I have a proposition to put to you in return for saving your life.

Twanky Where am I? Oh, Aladdin, you're safe. Hello, Alfonso.

Abanazer ABANAZER!

Aladdin Uncle Ebuchanezzer saved my life.

Twanky Oh, thank you.

Abanazer MY NAME IS – oh, never mind. Will you come with me to hear my proposition?

Aladdin Oh, very well. It's the least I can do. See you later.

Abanazer *and* **Aladdin** *exit.*

Twanky Oh, he's such a nice man. And wealthy too. He seems to be the only one around here with any money. Hey, shall we have some fun with this lot?

Wishee What a good idea.

They set up statues in a line in funny shapes with **Empress** *at end of line.*

Twanky Ready?

Wishee Yes.

Twanky *pushes/kicks the first one and they rush off. It goes along line and ends with* **Emperor** *kicking* **Empress** *up bottom and she shoots off-stage.*

Curtain.

End of Scene Three

Scene Four

All in front of tabs as stage prepared for magic cave and transformation.

Enter **Aladdin** *and* **Abanazer**, *with skulls in his belt.*

Aladdin I'm still not sure that this is a good idea. The mountains are very wild and dangerous. Besides, I want to stay near the Princess.

Abanazer You ungrateful boy. I save your life and ask a favour in return. You impudent infidel.

Aladdin Now, there's no need to get personal. I know it seems a bit ungrateful, but at the moment I have much more important things to do.

Abanazer You must help me find the magic cave. *(aside)* This lad is becoming a nuisance. He will do what I want. *(to* **Aladdin***)* Now look here, you come from a fairly poor family, yes?

Aladdin Poor, but honest.

Abanazer And what chance do you have of marrying the Princess? They want somebody who has plenty of money, and who is a prince.

Aladdin I don't know. I'm not doing bad so far!

Abanazer BAD? BAD? How bad is nearly having your head chopped off? If you come with me and help me find the magic cave I will make sure you come back rich.

Aladdin Oh, you will, will you? I suppose money grows on trees in this magic cave?

Abanazer How dare you question my ability. I am the greatest magician in the world.

Aladdin Oh, yes? Well prove it!

Abanazer The impudence of this scoundrel knows no bounds. Very well, watch.

He does some fairly impressive trick; possibly with a large mirror turned at 45 degrees in gap in curtains and **Twanky's** *reflection.*

Aladdin Well, I must confess that was not bad, but I once saw Paul Daniels saw someone in half.

Abanazer That could be arranged if you persist with this awkwardness.

Aladdin Oh, no, you don't. I've somewhere to go. Bye.

Aladdin *slips off.*

Abanazer Curses! Curses! This boy is proving more difficult than expected.
(*timp under these lines*)
Aladdin will not take the bait
So the Great Abanazer has to wait
But my time will come before too long
I'll have him in my power anon
He'll take me to the magic cave
So his life and fortunes he can save
What he doesn't know is that when he's done

The magic cave will become his tomb
Ha ha ha ha ha ha!

Evil laugh gets boos out of audience. **Abanazer** *reacts to them and they boo louder.*

Silence you [Halifax] boo boys. You can't beat the Great Abanazer. *(He snarls at audience)* Poor Aladdin.
By that which burns beneath the sky
He'll take me to the magic cave and DIE!!!

Brings a further torrent of boos from the audience.

Twanky *enters.*

Twanky What on earth is going on here. *(looks around)* They don't seem to like you very much, do they? What are they cross about?

Abanazer Oh. I was just telling them a little bedtime story. Isn't that right?

Audience NO!!

Abanazer But now you're here, I have a proposition for you.

Twanky Oh! *(flutters her eyes, straightens her hair and frock)* What could that be?

Abanazer I have brought some souvenirs from Arabia. Look at this. *(takes of one of the skulls)* This is the skull of the Great Queen Boadicea. How would you like to buy it?

Twanky Hmm, it would look quite fetching on my mantelpiece. Good looking woman, wasn't she? Is it genuine?

Abanazer Of course, it is. Absolutely genuine.

Twanky Well, how much do you want for it?

Abanazer As it's a real collector's piece, to you – twenty pounds.

Twanky Twenty pounds? That's a lot of money. I don't think I can afford it.

Abanazer Well, what about this one then, this is cheaper. This is Queen Boadicea's skull when she was a girl. Only five pounds.

Twanky Oh, I'll have that one.

She digs out some money from her bloomers. She hands over the money.

Twanky Thank you very much. *(walks slowly to exit)*

Abanazer *(pockets the money)* Thank you, dear lady. Indeed a bargain. *(makes a devious gloating exit, opposite side)*

Twanky *(stops suddenly, realises)* When she was a girl? Hey, hey, come back. I've been diddled. Hey, Have a banana, come back here.

Twanky exits following **Abanazer**.

Enter **Princess** *and* **Aladdin**.

Princess You know how dangerous it is for us to be together.

Aladdin I know, but for Uncle Abanazer I wouldn't be here now.

Princess Well, I want you to take this ring and wear it always.

Aladdin Oh, I couldn't. It looks very expensive.

Princess It is a very old ring that has been in my family for many generations. It is said to be able to help the wearer if they are a danger. I would like you to wear it and then it might save you one day.

Aladdin That is very sweet of you. I'm afraid I can't give you anything in return, except my love.

Princess That is more than enough.

SONG
PRODUCTION NUMBER
Princess *and* Aladdin

After applause, much shouting from offstage.
Chop Suey, Chow Mein, Vizir *and* **Executioner** *run on.*

Vizir Capture him, and don't let him escape this time.

> **Princess** *screams as* **Chop Suey** *and* **Chow Mein** *grab* **Aladdin***.* **Vizir** *moves to* **Princess***.*

Vizir You are safe now, Lotus Blossom.

Princess I was safe before. Please let him go.

Vizir Let him go? My dear, this lad is dangerous and must be dealt with severely. And remember your father's proclamation. You will be far safer when you marry my son, Prince Pekoe.

Princess But I don't want to marry Pekoe.

Vizir My dear, you are upset and hysterical. Come along with me. Bring the prisoner to the palace. Do not let him escape.

__Vizir__ and __Princess__ exit. __Aladdin__ is struggling as they try to take him off.

Aladdin Unhand me, let go. Help! Help! Uncle Abanazer, save me.

__Abanazer__ enters.

Abanazer Yes, Aladdin. What is it?

Aladdin Help me Uncle Abanazer, please. They are going to take me to the palace.

Abanazer I don't know whether I should help you. You wouldn't help me.

Aladdin Oh, I will, I will. Please help me. I will go with you to the cave.

Abanazer Very well, I shall help you again.
Spirits, demons, spectres and ghosts,
Come to haunt our unwelcome hosts,
Confuse the captors, make them harassed,
To take the wrong one back to the palace.

As he says this spell, he waves his arms around. They let go of __Aladdin__ and take hold of __Executioner__ and with a struggle, take him offstage.

Abanazer Once more, Aladdin, I've managed to save,
　　Take me at once to the magic cave.

Aladdin Very well, this way. Will I ever see this place again?

　　Abanazer *and* **Aladdin** *exit.*

<u>End of Scene Four</u>

Scene Five

Tabs still closed. Dance in front of tabs (possibly animals, demons, etc. U.V.s) End of dance, spooky music. **Abanazer** *and* **Aladdin** *enter through auditorium side door and they walk round hall through following lines.*

Abanazer Now, come along, we've been up and down Khyber Pass three times now. Where is this magic cave?

Aladdin I know it's here – somewhere near here. But I'm tired now. We've been walking for days. I want a rest.

Abanazer A rest? A rest? The boy's a lazy, idle, good-for-nothing idiot. We are not going to rest when we are so near. You can rest as much as you like when we get to the magic cave. *(laughs sneeringly)*

Aladdin I don't like this. I wish I'd never come. *(to audience)* Do you wish you hadn't come as well? You must be mad!!

While **Abanazer** *and* **Aladdin** *are out in hall, curtains open slightly to reveal boulder over cave entrance.*

Abanazer If we do not find this cave soon, the smell of five thousand camels will pervade your nostrils forever. You will be tied in a pit with twenty constipated elephants and time will take its course!

Aladdin No, no, not that! The cave must be very near. Look! There it is.

They go up on to stage.

Abanazer At last! This is what I have dreamed of for years! Inside that cave is treasure beyond imagination. But more important is a lamp... A lamp that will make all my ambitions come true. I shall be the most powerful man in the whole world. *(He gloats, audience boo)*

Aladdin Now he thinks he's [Michelle Barnier].

Abanazer I shall control everything and everyone.

Aladdin No, it's...

Abanazer I shall have all the money in all the world.

Aladdin Could be [Mark Zuckerberg].

Abanazer Enough of this fooling! There's no time to waste. Open the cave!

Aladdin Me? Don't be silly. It's got to be opened by some secret words. Don't you know?

Abanazer I used to... *(thinks)* ...but I can't remember... *(thinks)*

Aladdin Well, that's it then, so much for your dreams. "I'm going to be the most powerful man in the world"!! And you've dragged us all the way up here and forgotten the secret words! I'm off home.

Abanazer No, wait!! Someone must know the secret words. *(to audience)* Does anyone know the story of the magic cave?

Audience *(little response)*

Aladdin Does anybody know the password?

Audience Yes!

Abanazer *(getting excited)* You do? What is it? What? Shout louder. Old Man Zebedee? No, that doesn't sound right.

Aladdin Open Saturday? What? Can't hear. Look all together, after three. One, two, three...

Audience OPEN SESAME!!

They turn round and see the boulder roll aside.

Abanazer Wonderful! Right, off you go!

Aladdin Ta! I'm ready for a cuppa! *(turns to exit)*

Abanazer Hey, hang on!! Where are you going?

Aladdin Home. I've finished now, haven't I?

Abanazer Certainly not! I can't get in here. I'm much too big. You'll have to go in!

Aladdin Oh, I will, will I? Who says so?

Abanazer I say so!

Abanazer *makes magic pass at* **Aladdin** *who goes into a trance. He makes some indications to show* **Aladdin** *is obedient.*

Abanazer That should do the trick long enough for me to get what I want.

Abanazer *"arranges"* **Aladdin's** *exit through opening into cave set. Curtains close over next few lines.*

Abanazer Ha, ha, ha!!

Now my scheme is really working
The magic lamp within this cave
Will soon be all mine for the taking
And make the wealth for this poor knave. Ha ha.
This fool Aladdin knows not what his fate is
In blissful ignorance he will sigh
He'll never again know just what day it is
For inside this cave he'll wither and DIE!!
Ha, ha, ha, ha, ha!!

Abanazer *exits to go round back of stage.*

Curtains open slowly on cave. **Aladdin** *is in darkness, walking down from back corner.*

Aladdin Gosh, this is spooky. Ugh, spiders. I hate spiders. I hate caves come to that. How did I get in here? My head feels funny.

Abanazer *(He has arrived behind small opening in back corner)* CURSES!! My spell is wearing off already. He's waking up. Aladdin, Aladdin. Can you see the lamp down there?

Aladdin I can see hundreds and hundreds of jewels. They must be worth a fortune. There's diamonds, rubies, emeralds.

Abanazer You can have all the jewels you want but find the lamp!

Aladdin Just a minute.

Abanazer Just a minute? Just a minute? You are a thoroughly unhelpful person, and I am running out of patience.

Aladdin Don't shout at me like that.

Abanazer Well, find the lamp.

Aladdin I can't see anything down here, it's so dark.

Abanazer Well, look around!

Aladdin Why do you want this lamp so much?

Abanazer Never mind that. Just find it!

Aladdin You're not bothered about these jewels, are you?

Abanazer No!!

Aladdin You just want the lamp?

Abanazer Yes!

Aladdin And I can have the jewels?

Abanazer As many as you want.

Aladdin Then what's so special about the lamp?

Abanazer Mind your own business!

Aladdin It is my business. I'm the one that's stuck down here. Hey, you're not going to leave me down here, are you?

Abanazer To think I could do such a thing! Now, give me that lamp!!

Aladdin I haven't found it yet. Oh, what's this? You can't mean THIS rusty old thing?

Abanazer Yes, yes, that's it, that's it. Give it to me... PLEASE!!

Aladdin What on earth can he possibly want with THIS battered old thing? Methinks there is more to this than meets the eye. *(to audience)* Do you think I should give him the lamp?

Audience NO!!

Aladdin Is it very valuable, then?

Audience YES!!

Aladdin Oh, well, if you say so. I'm going to keep the lamp.

Abanazer I'll give you one last chance to save yourself, or spend your last days in this cave rotting.

Aladdin Are you sure I should keep the lamp?

Audience YES!!

Aladdin I hope you're right, that's all. No, uncle, I'm keeping the lamp.

Abanazer CURSES! CURSES! Well, you asked for it.
Aladdin Twanky your days are ended
For foolishness you'll be remembered
They'll never find you right out here
You'll rot for ever, year after year.

Aladdin No! No!

Abanazer The rats and mice will accompany you
Your last breath will soon be overdue
I say goodbye, this lonely cave
Will turn out to be a suitable grave.
KALAKAZAM!!

Sound of stone rolling back and **Abanazer** *disappears from view and "hole" covers up.*

Aladdin *(nervously)* Uncle! Uncle!! Oh, what am I going to do? There is no way out of here. What a silly thing to do! I can't understand all this. *(sits down on something, clutching lamp)* All because of this stupid lamp. *(rustling noise is heard)*

Aagh! Mice or rats, OR WORSE!! Oh, Uncle. Come back! *(runs to back corner)* HELP! HELP! *(comes back to sit down)* Oh, it's hopeless. *(stands up, goes to the audience)* What can I do?

Audience Rub the lamp.

Aladdin What did you say? Rub the lamp? Oh well, here goes.

Aladdin *rubs the lamp. Flash, smoke and* **Genie** *appears.* **Aladdin** *is suitably surprised.*

Genie I am the Genie of the Lamp. Your wish is my command, O Master.

Aladdin You are who?

Genie I am the Genie of the Lamp. I will grant any of your wishes. The one who rubs the lamp to summon the Genie is my master.

Aladdin No wonder Uncle Abanazer wanted the lamp. Can you grant any wishes?

Genie Any wishes at your command, O Master?

Aladdin Can I have a drink, please?

Genie At once.

*Genie claps his hands and **Genie's Assistant** comes on with a tray and two glasses and a bottle of Lucozade.*

Aladdin Thank you, would you like one?

Genie Thank you, O Master. I have been in that lamp for a long time.

*They both take a drink. **Assistant** takes away tray and glasses.*

Aladdin Ah, that's better. Now, to business. I need riches and clothes so that I can go back to Peking and marry my princess.

Genie Your wish is my command!

*Genie claps his hands. Music starts. Light effects and transformation as **dancers** come in with jewelled boxes etc. Centre piece opens up to reveal treasure chest containing gold and silver and jewels etc. **Aladdin** changes costume to rich clothes during ballet and dance ends with posed tableau.*

MUSIC
PRODUCTION NUMBER

Aladdin And now, back to Peking.

Genie My Master commands and I obey.

> **Genie** *makes magical passes. Light effects, wind noise as curtains close on tableau.*

<u>End of Scene Five</u>

<u>END OF ACT ONE</u>

<u>INTERVAL</u>

ACT
TWO

Scene Six

Outside **Widow Twanky's** *laundry. Laundry front set to one side, across rear opening, with a practical door. Remainder of backboard painted with sky and a cut-out skyline resting against backboard allows the magic palace to be created later in scene.*

BRIGHT OPENING PRODUCTION NUMBER

Twanky, Wishee *and* **dancers**.

Posed ending, **dancers** *exit.*

Wishee HELLO, FOLKS.

Audience *(little reaction)*

Wishee Oh, do you know? We've only been off the air 20 minutes and they've gone off the boil already – or maybe it's the tea and biscuits. I didn't have any biscuits. **I** know where they've been! Now, come on, let's have another go. HELLO, FOLKS!!

Audience HELLO, WISHEE!

Wishee That's absolutely amazeballs! What do you think of the show so far?

Audience RUBBISH.

Twanky Well, it's not going to get any better!.

Wishee It's boring without Aladdin here. I'm fed up.

Twanky I know! I'll read us a story. I got a new book from the library, but I read so slowly I'm 50 pence overdue already and I'm only halfway through. Are you sitting comfortably? **(Wishee** *nods)* Then I'll begin. *(She reads)* I was on this case...

Wishee It had to be a case, I couldn't afford a desk. Ha! ha!

Twanky There was a tap on the door...

Wishee Funny place to put a tap!

Twanky There stood a redhead...

Wishee No hair, just a red head.

Twanky A tall blonde walked past the window...

Wishee She had to be tall, we were on the fourth floor.

Twanky Isn't it exciting.

Wishee If you like that sort of thing.

Twanky *(reads on)* A taxi pulled up with a jerk...

Wishee The jerk got out and we got in.

Twanky We walked into this bar...

Wishee OUCH!! It was an iron bar. *(holds a hand to his face)*

Twanky A woman rolled her eyes at me...

Wishee So, I picked them up and rolled them back to her.

Twanky *angrily closes book, traps her fingers.*

Twanky Ooooh! You're just not playing the game.

Wishee No, but it sounds like he is!!

Twanky Oh, you're impossible. Go and take that washing back to [Norma Bateman], then I can read my book in peace!

Wishee Do you know, you remind me of the Mona Lisa when you get cross.

Twanky I take it you mean beautiful and seductive.

Wishee No, flat and boring and you belong in a museum!!

Twanky GET OUT!!

Wishee GOING!

Wishee *exits with washing parcel.*

Vaudeville villain music as **Abanazer** *enters to boos. He has a very serious expression.*

Twanky Oh, I say he's back again. I wonder if we're rich. *(She prepares herself)* Er... Hello again. Is Aladdin following on behind? He's always slow, that one. *(She peers offstage)* I was in labour three weeks with him. I suppose he'll be coming any minute.

Abanazer I don't think so. He's not coming back.

Twanky You what? He hasn't got himself lost again has he?

Abanazer No, he's run away with all the jewels.

Twanky He's run away?

Abanazer Yes.

Twanky With all the jewels?

Abanazer YES! We found the cave… Aladdin went inside… he found the jewels… and he ran off with them. *(to audience)* He did, didn't he?

Audience No.

Abanazer Oh, yes he did!

Audience Oh, no he didn't!

Abanazer Oh, yes he did!

Audience OH, NO HE DIDN'T!

Abanazer Oh, yes he did!

    Aladdin *enters.*

Audience } OH, NO HE DIDN'T!
Aladdin   } OH, NO I DIDN'T!

Abanazer YOU!

Aladdin Yes, me! And you'd better scarper quick – or else!

Abanazer You'll not get away with this! I shall return and I shall get my just deserts.

Aladdin You'll get your just deserts all right. Most people get their just deserts in Heaven. You'll get yours in He… [Heckmondwike]! Get off!! *(to audience)* Come on, OFF, OFF, OFF, OFF, OFF.

    Abanazer *exits shaking his fist and snarling.*

Twanky Would someone mind telling me what's going on?

Aladdin "Uncle Abanazer" is a first-class villain. He left me trapped in the magic cave to die!!

Twanky The nasty piece of work!! It doesn't surprise me though! I wasn't fooled. I thought there was something funny about him all along. Anyway, where did you get all those posh clothes from? You look like a fancy-dress shop. Have you been shopping on Ebay?

Aladdin You wouldn't believe what I've got!

Twanky That's probably true.

Aladdin I've got jewels. Look. *(gets jewels from his pockets and gives them to* **Twanky** *as they sing to "I've got Rhythm")* We'll never have to work again. And I'll be able to marry Princess Lotus Blossom.

Twanky Are you sure these are real?

Aladdin Of course, they're real, and worth a fortune... BUT!!

Twanky What?

Aladdin More important!!

Twanky What? Don't keep me in suspenders!!

Aladdin Ta-rah! *(brandishes the magic lamp)*

Twanky *(not impressed)* What on earth is that?

Aladdin This is the magic lamp that Abanazer was so anxious to get his hands on.

Twanky More fool him. It's horrible!

Aladdin It's certainly not that! Here, *(gives her the lamp)* give it a rub.

Twanky A rub! It wants a right good clean up!! *(She rubs the lamp.* **Genie** *appears in effects. She screams)* It's Tinky Winky!!

Genie I am the Genie of the Lamp. Your wish is my command, O Mistress.

Twanky CHEEKY! *(aside to* **Aladdin***)* Who is he?

Aladdin He will grant your wishes.

Twanky Any wishes?

Genie Anything at all. I am here to serve you.

She smiles cheekily at the audience.

Aladdin Now, behave yourself.

Twanky I wish I could have a new frock.

Genie You command and I obey.

He claps his hands and **dancer** *comes in wearing Scene Five costume with glamorous dress.*

Twanky Oh, I'm flabbergasted. *(She puts dress on with* **dancer's** *help)* My flabber has never been so gasted. Bring Wishee Washee!

Genie At once!

Wishee *enters as if dragged on.*

Wishee HELLO, FOLKS!

Audience HELLO, WISHEE!

Wishee What's going on here? It looks like you've been to Primark. *(sees* **Genie***)* Eeeek!

Aladdin We have made our fortunes at last – with the help of this fellow. He can grant any wishes! We will be rich and famous, and I shall be able to marry the Princess.

Enter **Chop Suey** *and* **Chow Mein**, *dramatically.*

Chop Suey *(very thespian)* We have come to arrest Aladdin.

Chow Mein *(tries to copy)* We have come to arrest Aladdin.

Wishee You'll have to get past me first.

Chop Suey *and* **Chow Mein** *advance.*

Wishee Oh, very well! There he is!

Twanky Oh, Aladdin, do something. *(***Aladdin** *does a quick shuffle hop step)*

Chop Suey It's no good, we've got our orders.

Chow Mein It's no good, we've got our odours.

Wishee Well, bring me a pint, I'm thirsty.

Chow Mein Good idea!

Twanky Mine's a light!

Chow Mein Quick someone get a bucket of water!

Chop Suey *(to* **Chow Mein***)* You are a fool. You are stupid. *(smacks his face on letters)* S-T-U-P-I-D, stupid.

Chow Mein Well, you're incompetent. *(smacks* **Chop's** *face)* I-N-K- *(stops to think)* I-N-K-O- *(stops again)* D-A-F-T, daft.

Chop Suey Just you wait till we get back.

Aladdin You are not going to arrest me.

Chop Suey Oh, we're not, aren't we?

Chow Mein We're not?

Aladdin I am now the richest man in Peking. Richer than [Richard Branson].

Chop Suey Richer than [Bill Gates]?

Chow Mein Richer than [Donald Trump]?

Aladdin Richer than all of them put together.

Chop Suey }
Chow Mein } WOW!!

Aladdin Now this is what you WILL do! Go back to the palace and ask the Emperor to come down here at once, when he will hear something to his advantage.

Chop Suey Hey! We're not your lackeys.

Aladdin Genie!!

    Genie *moves across and menaces them with his height.*

Chop Suey Very well, just this once. Come on fish face.

Chop Suey *and* **Chow Mein** *exit.*

Twanky Do you think Genie ought to go back in the lamp?

Aladdin What?

Twanky *(mimes)* Genie back in lamp.

Genie *(looks intently at his height and at lamp)* If it's all the same to you I'll wait outside. I've been in there for thousands of years.

Aladdin Well, don't go away.

Genie Never fear, Genie's here. Your wish is my command, O Master.

Genie *bows low and exits.*

Twanky Isn't this exciting. Riches – fame. We'll be in the royal family. There'll be hundreds of men chasing after me now. I needn't bother with the lonely hearts club now.

Aladdin The lonely hearts?

Twanky Yes. I keep sending them my photograph and they keep sending it back saying they're not THAT lonely.

Enter **Chop Suey** *and* **Chow Mein**.

Chop Suey The Emperor of Peking... *(fanfare)*

Chow Mein ...and Mrs Emperor. *(poor fanfare)*

Emperor *and* **Empress** *enter followed by* **Vizir**.

Empress I think this is rather too much, Ying Tong. The Emperor being summoned to a Chinese laundry. And remember what happened last time we were here.

Emperor Now, my precious little Ping Pong, I understand it to be to our advantage. And if it's not, we'll have their heads chopped off!!

Twanky Ah, thank you so much for accepting our invitation.

Empress It had better be worth the trouble.

Aladdin It certainly is! Due to happy circumstances beyond my control, I find myself embarrassed by untold wealth.

Empress *(they are both very interested)* Do you now?

Emperor You do? *(smiling all over)*

Aladdin It occurred to me that it may be to our mutual advantage *(digs **Twanky**)* to make a substantial investment in the royal coffers.

Emperor This sounds like a business proposition.

Aladdin Well, it's more of a marriage proposition. I wish to marry **the Princess**.

Empress WHAT?

Vizir NEVER!

Emperor QUIET! Go on young man.

Aladdin Let me show you.

Aladdin *rubs the lamp. Flash.* **Genie** *staggers on holding a beer bottle, obviously the worse for drink.*

Twanky Good Grief, he's sozzled!

Wishee It's the Genie with the light brown ale!! Ha, ha!

Aladdin What on earth have you been doing?

Genie I've been (hic) across the road in the Flying Scotsman mixing with the other spirits.

Twanky Dutchman!!

Genie Please yourself. *(Hic) (He lifts bottle to his mouth.* **Aladdin** *takes it and throws it into wings)*

Aladdin I think we caught him in the nick of time. Apologies, Your Majesties. It's a long time since he had a drink and he's not used to modern brews. *(to* **Genie***)* Pull yourself together. *(***Genie** *sways around,* **Twanky** *goes to hold him up)* Now Genie, bring some gold and jewels for the Emperor and Empress.

Genie Jold and Gewels?

Aladdin Gold and jewels, you big nit – and quick.

Genie *(bows unsteadily)* Your wind is my cushion. *(claps his hands and misses. Tries again and misses. Whistles instead. Tinkling music as girls bring on two caskets of jewels)*

Emperor Very impressive. And there are more of these?

Vizir Your Majesty, remember, the Princess is betrothed to my son, Pekoe.

Emperor It's off!

Vizir It's off?

Empress It's off!! *(***Emperor** *and* **Empress** *high five)*

Emperor He'll make a fine son-in-law.

    Vizir *storms off.*

Empress But where will you live? You can't bring the Princess to live here.

Aladdin I quite agree. Genie, I want a wonderful palace to be built over yonder, a palace surpassed in its excellence only by the Emperor's palace.

Genie At once, O Master. *(Hic)* You command and I obey.

    He manages to clap his hand. Wind, sound, strobe. Palace is flown to sit on landscape at back.

Twanky That's amazing! He builds houses faster than [Percy Simmons]. Other house builders are available!!

Emperor Come along, young man. Let's break the good news to the Princess.

Curtain starts to close. **Wishee** *and* **Twanky** *in front, others behind. Time curtains to close fully just after* **Genie's** *line.*

Aladdin Now, you can get back in there, then we know where you are.

Genie You command and I obey.

    Curtain.

Scene change to **Aladdin's** *palace.*

Twanky It's wonderful to see all these jewels, but it's true what they say. Diamonds are a girl's best friend.

SONG AND DANCE
"DIAMONDS ARE A GIRL'S BEST FRIEND"

Twanky, Wishee *and* **dancers**

End of Scene Six

Scene Seven

Inside **Aladdin's** *palace. Palace set in full stage with table and seating for five people. Tabs closed. Strobe set for later in scene.*

Abanazer *enters in front of tabs to boos from audience.*

Abanazer Quiet, you troublesome mob! QUIET! *(plays to audience as noise increases. Sneers)* Ha ha ha ha, you think I'm beaten, do you? Well, let me tell you, or you, or even you. I will get even with Aladdin. He'll not get away with trying to trick me. He's been very lucky so far – and so have you, you lily livered morons!

PRODUCTION NOTE: If required a special effect magic trick, possibly in strobe could be used here, for effect or to give longer for scene change.

Abanazer *takes up imposing sinister stance, centre stage.*

You will see. My time is nigh. I'll defeat Aladdin, and HE WILL DIE!! Ha ha ha ha ha ha!!

Sinister guffaws build up until he is laughing strongly, provoking large reaction from audience, draws it out and then, with a flash of his cloak, disappears at corner exit.

As lights return to normal, Chinese tinkling is heard and curtains open on palace. **Aladdin** *and* **Princess** *are on stage.*

Princess I am so happy. This palace is absolutely wonderful and shortly we shall be husband and wife, prince and princess.

Aladdin Prince Aladdin. Yes, it's certainly got a ring to it. But did you have to invite your parents and my mother today?

Princess Of course. It is the Chinese custom that prospective in-laws inspect the matrimonial home before the wedding.

Aladdin Who am I to interfere with Chinese customs?

Enter **Sing Hi, Sing Lo** *and* **Pekoe.**

Sing Hi Oh, Princess, I am so happy for you.

Princess I suspect that you are equally happy for yourself, and so am I.

Sing Hi Thank you, Princess. Now the intended marriage between you and Prince Pekoe is officially off, we can be happy together.

Pekoe Yes, I wish for nothing more. Yet my father, the Vizir, is still not going to be very happy about it. He wants me to marry someone who is in royal circles – and rich.

Aladdin Do not worry, my friend. We will help you and I think you will find things a lot easier than you imagine. I think the Vizir will be quite satisfied eventually.

Pekoe I hope so.

Sing Lo I think we will all be very happy. *(shyly)* I think Wishee Washee is quite fond of me.

Aladdin I'm sure he is. He talks of nothing else.

Sing Lo Oh really? *(fluttering eyelashes)* I am so lucky. He really is a very nice young man.

Aladdin It's in the blood.

Pekoe And very soon we will all be able to be together.

Aladdin Yes, but even sooner the Emperor and Empress will be coming, so we must prepare ourselves.

Pekoe Quite so. *(to **Sing Hi**)* I will see you very soon.

Sing Hi I will see you out. Come this way.

> ***Sing Hi** and **Pekoe** exit.*

> *Doorbell sound or fanfare.*

Aladdin Oh well, here they are.

> ***Sing Lo** goes to door and returns with **Emperor**, **Empress** and **Twanky**, who is dressed in the loudest, gaudiest costume and wig. **Emperor** and **Empress** are continually embarrassed and exasperated through this next piece.*

Twanky Hello again, Ying and Ping! You don't mind me calling you Ying and Ping, do you? I think it is important to get off on the right foot!

> ***Twanky** stands on **Emperor's** foot.*

Emperor *(jumps about)* Ow! ow! ow!

Aladdin That's getting off on the right foot alright! Would you like some tea?

Empress That would be very nice.

Twanky Oh, dee-lightful darling. What a SPLENDID idea!!

Princess *(to* **Sing Lo***)* Will you arrange tea, please?

> **Princess** *beckons to* **Sing Lo** *to get* **Sing Hi** *from other exit.* **Sing Lo** *and* **Sing Hi** *cross stage and exit.* **Aladdin** *is telling* **Twanky** *off.*

Princess Please sit down.

> **Empress** *sits down,* **Emperor** *goes to sit down, but* **Twanky** *pinches his chair and he falls on floor, legs in air. They rush to get him to his feet and get in a muddle. They dust him down.*

Twanky Don't worry about that little mark, Ying dear. Just pop it round to the laundry tomorrow.

> **Sing Hi** *and* **Sing Lo** *enter with trays on which are teapot, cups, saucers, etc. Put trays on table, bow and exit. Everybody is now seated.*

Emperor Did you hear about Hoo Flung Wen, the sugar producer? His wife is expecting.

> **Princess** *has been passing cups out.* **Empress** *passes over sugar bowl.*

Empress One lump or two?

Twanky Ooooh, ha ha ha! *(She nudges the **Emperor** as he is drinking. He splutters)* One lump or two!! *(She is in hysterics, everyone else is straight-faced. She stops laughing suddenly)* Oh, please yourselves. *(to **Empress**)* By the way, Happy Birthday for tomorrow.

Empress That's very thoughtful of you, I'm touched.

Twanky I've often thought that!!

Aladdin Mother!! Behave and drink your tea.

Twanky Hey!! Something just struck me.

Empress *(loud aside to **Emperor**)* Something is about to!!

Twanky We will be related soon, won't we? *(suitable looks from **Emperor** and **Empress** and they both take a drink of tea - and a tablet?)* There's nothing I like better than having relations. Don't you agree?

Empress Er – er – er, HEAVENS!!

Princess What's the matter?

Empress We will have to go.

Twanky Oh? So soon? I was just beginning to get into my stride.

Empress Yes, I can see that! Well, it's been lovely. We'll look forward to the wedding. Come along Ying Tong.

> **Emperor** and **Empress** kiss **Princess** on cheek, shake **Aladdin's** hand. He kisses **Empress's** hand. They turn to **Twanky**, pause and exit.

Twanky What lovely people. I hope I made a good impression.

Aladdin Well, you made an impression alright!!

Twanky I think I'd better go now and see what Wishee is up to in the laundry. I'll see you shortly.

She goes to **Princess** *and kisses her warmly on cheek, throws her arms around* **Aladdin** *in a bear hug, he coughs and splutters.* **Twanky** *exits,* **Princess** *and* **Aladdin** *collapse in chairs.*

Aladdin I hope future family gatherings will not be as bad as that one.

Princess Oh, don't worry. I'm sure they will all get on fine before long. They have to get used to each other.

Aladdin I suppose you're right. Well, I think I should go and finalise the wedding arrangements for tomorrow.

Princess I will stay here for a while with Sing Hi and Sing Lo. I have nearly got everything ready. We are so lucky, aren't we?

Aladdin I am!! *(He kisses* **Princess's** *cheek).* I will see you tomorrow.

Princess You certainly will.

Aladdin and **Princess** *exit.* **Sing Hi** *and* **Sing Lo** *enter and start clearing tea things away.* **Sing Hi** *takes them off during next lines.* **Abanazer's** *voice is heard offstage.*

Abanazer *(offstage)* New lamps for old! New lamps for old!

Sing Lo *goes to other door and returns alone.*

Sing Lo Princess, Princess! There is an old peddler at the door exchanging new lamps for old ones.

Princess *enters.*

Princess That sounds rather a strange way to do business!

Abanazer *(still offstage)* New lamps for old! New lamps for old!!

Princess We may as well have a look at what he has. Let him in.

Sing Lo *exits and re-enters followed by* **Abanazer** *in a cloak and hood. He looks and leers at audience who will boo.*

Abanazer New lamps for old, my dear. Lovely new shiny lamps.

Princess Isn't it odd to give away new things in exchange for old things?

Abanazer Well, my dear, I am a rich eccentric who likes to bring a little light into peoples' dull lives. *(glares at the audience)* I'm sure you would be pleased with one of these brand-new lamps, wouldn't you?

Princess *(looks)* Well, they look very fine. Do they work?

Abanazer Of course, they work. Look. See how that shines? And look. I have one of the famous magic lamps. *(He produces light bulb and makes it light, lights having dimmed a little)*

Princess That's marvellous! Aladdin has some sort of a lamp, but it doesn't seem to light up.

Abanazer He does? Well, there you are, my dear. What a lovely surprise it will be. Think how much that will please him.

Princess Sing Lo, please fetch that dirty lamp from Aladdin's study.

Sing Lo *exits.*

Abanazer Here you are, my dear. A lovely new lamp. *(He turns to audience as* **Princess** *looks at new lamp. Aside)* And in a moment I will have the REAL magic lamp. You see you horrible monsters. I told you no-one can trick ME and get away with it.

Sing Lo *enters with the lamp.*

Sing Lo I'm not sure this is a good idea, Princess.

Princess Nonsense, Sing Lo. Aladdin will be delighted. *(to audience)* Won't Aladdin be pleased?

Audience NO!!

Princess Don't you think I should give the lamp to this nice old man for a new one?

Abanazer *nods at the audience.*

Audience NO!!

Princess Oh, I'm sure you must be wrong. Here you are.

Abanazer takes the lamp.

Abanazer HA HA!! *(**Princess** is startled)*. At last, in my own hands .... THE MAGIC LAMP!!

He puts other lamps down or throws into wings.

Princess What do you mean?

Abanazer I mean, my dear... *(stands up straight and removes his hood)* ...that you and Aladdin have been tricked. HA HA HA HA HA!!

Abanazer *grabs* **Princess**, *rubs the lamp,* **Genie** *appears,* **Princess** *screams.*

Genie I am the Genie of the lamp. Your wish is my command, O Master.

Abanazer *(during this speech the lights dim and flash and strobe lights)*
At last I have you in my power
The witches and the spirits cower
Make Aladdin's palace and all that's within
Disappear to a place that man has never been – for long!!

Genie You command and I obey. We go to the MOON!!

Wind noises, whistles, shouting, light effects etc. as curtains close.

Evil dance to end scene in front of tabs.

End of Scene Seven

Scene Eight

Outside **Widow Twanky's** *laundry. (Palace gone from scenery.)*

Curtain opens on **Twanky**, **Aladdin** *and* **Wishee** *who are in their poor costumes again, sat on a bench outside the laundry. All have their chins resting on one hand and their elbow resting on one knee, looking extremely sad and quiet. Following diction is spaced – lines, pause, lines pause, etc.*

Wishee *(fairly sadly)* HELLO, FOLKS!

Audience HELLO, WISHEE!

Twanky I thought it was too good to last.

Wishee I lost my girl before I got her.

Twanky It was nice, though… for a while.

Wishee I'd never known what it was like to be rich.

Twanky He's not saying much, is he?

Wishee I think he's gob-smacked!!

They all sigh in unison and change arms in unison.

Twanky We haven't had much custom since, have we?

Wishee They all think it's our fault.

Aladdin *opens his mouth, as if to speak, they look at him. All drop arms. He changes his mind; they all change arms again.*

Twanky Do you think he's a bit put out?

Wishee I think he is, just a little bit.

Aladdin *stands up. They look at him, then at each other, then they stand up as well.*

Twanky Has the Queen come in?

Aladdin *brushes down his clothes and sits down. They do the same and change arms again.*

Twanky *(stands up and shouts)* I CAN'T STAND IT!!

Wishee *pulls her down by her shoulder, they change arms again. They tut, change arms a few times, getting quicker,* **Twanky** *gets out of time eventually. Normal diction from now on.*

Twanky Look, we can't stay like this all the time. We've got to snap out of it. I'll tell you a joke. What's brown and can see just as well from either end?

Wishee I don't know. What is brown and can see just as well from either end?

Twanky A horse with its eyes shut.

They laugh.

Wishee I know a joke. I say, I say, I say.

Twanky What do you say?

Wishee What did one centipede say to the other centipede when a lady centipede walked past?

Twanky I don't know, what did one centipede say to the other centipede when a lady centipede walked past?

Wishee What a lovely pair of legs, pair of legs, pair of...

Twanky Come along Aladdin, join in. It's no good sitting and moping all the time. Cheer up and something will turn up.

Aladdin Oh, alright. I'll give it a try. I say I say, I say.

Wishee What do you say?

Aladdin What are hippies for?

Wishee I don't know, what are hippies for?

Aladdin To stop your leggies from falling over.

Twanky *(seriously excited)* I say, I say!!

Aladdin What do you say?

Twanky What did the Princess give you in Scene Four in case you were ever in trouble?

Aladdin I don't know, what did the Princess give me in Scene Four in case...

He stops suddenly.

Aladdin }
Twanky } THE RING!!
Wishee }

Aladdin But what do we do with it?

104

Twanky I don't know. Come on let's sit down and have a look at it.

They sit down on bench; lights dim or go out.

Fairy dance either in strobe or U.V. using rings as props. **Dancers** *exit after posed ending.*

Lights come up and the three come back to front of tabs which close.

Scene change to moon (Scene Nine).

Wishee I know this might sound a bit odd, but I bet our friends down there know what we should do with it, don't you?

Audience YES!

Twanky Well. What should we do with it? And if anybody's cheeky, they'll go out!

Audience Rub it.

Twanky Oh, that's novel!! Go on then, give it a rub!

Aladdin *does so, and* **Fairy Diamante** *appears amid special effects.*

Wishee Cor!! Some more rubbing magic! Who are you?

Fairy I am Fairy Diamante, the slave of the ring.

Aladdin Can you help us? My princess, her handmaidens and my palace have been taken away by the evil Abanazer, and we don't know where.

Fairy I do!

Twanky You do?

Fairy I do!

Wishee Talkative, isn't she? Where are they?

Fairy On the moon.

They all immediately look up.

Aladdin Up there?

Fairy That's right.

Wishee I hope he gets splattered by a spaceship!!

Twanky How are we going to get them down from up there?

Fairy We can't get them down. We are going to have to go up there. The Genie's powers are much stronger than mine.

Aladdin When can we go?

Fairy Well, there's no time like the present.

Wishee Can we all go?

Fairy Yes, if you wish to.

Aladdin All for one, and one for all?

All AYE!!

Aladdin Right, then, we're ready. I just hope we're not too late. What do we have to do?

Fairy Just close your eyes and wish. *(they do)*
Spirits that fly on the heavenly wing
Please give some help to this slave of the ring

We must go to the moon to help our princess
So we put to the test your astounding prowess
With hearts full of passion and nerves of steel
We commit ourselves with unlimited zeal
So bring us your charger that we may quite soon
Get set on our journey up there to the moon.

Doctor Who music plays and curtains partly open to reveal a Tardis painted on flat with a practical door.

Wishee *(looking around)* What's all this? We're still here. That wasn't a very good spell.

Twanky What are we going to do now?

Aladdin I must admit I'm a little disappointed.

Fairy *(to audience)* Tell them, will you? Go on, tell them.

(Audience shout out, "It's behind you!! Cast ad-lib, "What is it?" "A what", "I can't hear you", "Shout louder", "A parcel", "Where", etc., etc. till noise builds up)

Twanky *(sees Tardis, does a double take, screams, and backs away)* LOOK!!

Aladdin What's that?

Fairy That is our spaceship.

Aladdin I'm sorry we doubted you.

Fairy That's alright. Come on then, in you go.

They go through door in Tardis.

Fairy *(turns to audience as she exits last through Tardis door)* We'll see you on the moon!!

Noise of Tardis setting off. Flashing lights including blue lamp on top. Noise fades as curtains close.

End of Scene Eight

Scene Nine

In the Sea of Tranquillity on the moon.

Curtain opens on black painted/draped set with stars and the earth in the background. A view of part of the palace at side. **Abanazer** *is standing on stage in green spot and slowly walks forward, glaring, to boos from audience.*

Abanazer Ha ha ha ha ha!! *(sneering at audience)* They'll never find us up here on the moon. This is Abanazer's moon base in the Sea of Tranquillity. But there'll be no tranquillity for the Princess ...soon to be my wife. Ha ha ha ha ha!! Now there's a real Man in the Moon. Your bedtime stories won't be the same any more, thanks to your Uncle Abanazer. Ha ha ha!! *(draws boos from audience)* Bah, you lowly earthlings, you will rue the day that you abused the Great Abanazer – as Aladdin did, to his cost. That "poor" boy. He almost made his way into the Peking royal family – but for me!! The Greatest Magician in the world.

He takes up imposing position.

The sun and moon and earth and stars
Including that peculiar Mars
Can hold no candle 'gainst the man
Whose magic pervades this wonderland.
The princess locked in nearby palace
Has had her life put out of balance
But once again she'll happy be

'Cos very soon she'll marry me!!

Ha ha!! *(drawing boos from the audience.)*

Quiet you, your mangy mumblings

Respect your Master, stop your rumbling

Or you will find, as did Aladdin

That opposition makes you sadden

Admit defeat, the tears you're shedding

Must dry out soon – we're near the WEDDING.

Ha, ha ha ha ha!!! *(sweeps back and forth across stage to boos and hisses, then exits with a swirl of his cloak front left.* **Princess**, **Sing Hi** *and* **Sing Lo** *enter back left)*

Sing Lo Oh, Princess, what are we going to do?

Princess I don't know. We are trapped here. There is nowhere to escape to.

Sing Hi Mister Abanazer will be cross when he finds out we're not in the palace where he left us.

Sing Lo Well, he can't do much worse to us than he's already done. Here we are, thousands of miles away from home. All our people are over there. *(points to earth on scenery)* Oh, Princess, I'm frightened. *(cries)*

Princess Now, now, my dear. *(comforts* **Sing Lo***)* That isn't going to achieve anything, is it? I'm sure that Abanazer won't actually harm us.

Sing Hi That's as long as we do what he says. And he says he wants you to marry him.

Princess Yes, and he means it, too.

Sing Lo How horrible!

Sing Hi You mustn't Princess.

Princess I hate to admit it, but there doesn't seem to be any alternative.

Sing Lo I would rather die!

Princess That may be the alternative. Or he will use the Genie of the Lamp. Anyway, I cannot think of myself. I have to consider you, too.

Sing Hi No, Your Highness. We will serve you to the end!

Princess That is very sweet, Sing Hi. I am grateful for your support, but I won't risk your safety.

Abanazer enters back left and slowly moves down behind them over next few lines. These lines may be lost amid audience noise.

Sing Lo We can't give in to this man. He is an evil animal. We must fight him.

Sing Hi We won't let you down, Your Highness.

*Abanazer grabs hold of **Princess's** arm. They all react with surprise.*

Abanazer So very touching …and so very silly of you to leave the palace. You will all be punished, and that is a shame so near to our wedding.

Princess I shall not marry you. I demand that you take us back to Peking.

111

Abanazer *(laughs loudly)* Oh no! You will never get back to Peking. We will make a magnificent kingdom here on the moon, with the help of the Genie. And then we shall control all the earth from here. I shall be the most powerful man in the whole of space!

Princess You are insane. You'll not get away with this. **(Princess** *bites his hand)*

Abanazer Ow!!

Sing Hi *kicks his shin. He hops around.*

Abanazer Enough of this!! Come, into the palace. I think the sooner we get this marriage ceremony over, the happier we will be.

Princess The happier YOU may be, but you will be the only one.

Abanazer I'm sure you will find me a gentle, kind and considerate husband.

Princess }
Sing Hi } EUURGH!!
Sing Lo }

Abanazer By the spirits of the solar system
We'll open the treasure locker
The wedding ceremony will soon take place...

Princess You must be off your rocker!!

Abanazer I'm going to have to knock some of that spirit out of you. Come!!

Abanazer *drags Princess off.* **Sing Hi** *and* **Sing Lo** *follow nervously.*

Sing Lo I wonder where Luke Skywalker is now?

Sing Hi *and* **Sing Lo** *exit.*

Lights dim. We see flashing lights and hear sound effects as if Tardis is landing just off stage. **Fairy** *enters apprehensively, sees coast is clear and beckons to others. They enter with slow and accentuated up and down movements as if no gravity.*

MUSIC
"GROUND CONTROL TO MAJOR TOM"

They have full face (square) helmets on and backpacks like oxygen cylinders. Strobe stops, music fades and lights come up.

Aladdin *tries to talk to* **Twanky**, *but his voice is very muffled. She indicates she cannot understand. He repeats. She still can't understand. She takes off her helmet as* **Aladdin** *produces cards with one word written on each card. DON'T – TAKE – YOUR – HELMET – OFF.* **Twanky** *replies with cards, TOO – LATE – GOODBYE! She takes up dramatic pose.*

Fairy *(sniffs air)* I don't think you need worry. I think Abanazer has already used the Genie's power to put oxygen in the air.

Twanky *mimes "OK to take helmet off".* **Aladdin** *doesn't understand. She takes deep breath, mimes OK, then coughs and splutters.* **Fairy** *taps* **Aladdin** *and* **Wishee's**

helmets, points upwards and they get the message and take their helmets off.

Wishee HELLO, FOLKS!

Audience HELLO, WISHEE!

Aladdin There's oxygen in the air!

Fairy A present from the Genie, I think.

Wishee *(goes to stage side)* I don't believe it! You get graffiti everywhere.

Twanky What does it say?

Wishee Neil Armstrong woz here 1969.

Fairy Well, now that you're all safely here
With all my help. I know
There's nothing more that I can do
It's time for me to go.

Twanky You're not going to leave us, are you? We've only just got to know you!

Wishee Oh, please stay, we may need your help.

Fairy I can't compete with the Genie's powers. They are much stronger than mine. I am sure that with strength and perseverance...

Twanky Percy who?

Fairy Perseverance ...you will win through. It's over to you now. Goodbye and GOOD LUCK!!

*All say goodbyes as **Fairy** exits, cast waving. Tardis lights flash and noise fades away. Pause on stage.*

Wishee Well,... er... *(uncomfortably)* What are we going to do now? HEY! The palace is here, we've found it!

Aladdin We must find the Princess and Sing Hi and Sing Lo, make sure they are safe, outsmart Abanazer, capture the lamp and get the Genie to take us back to Peking.

Twanky *and* **Wishee** *clap, slap his back etc.* **Aladdin** *looks pleased.*

Twanky We'll wait here for you.

Wishee We'll stay here and hold the fort. Give us a call before you set off.

Aladdin This is a job for all of us!

Wishee *and* **Twanky** *look around.*

Twanky All of who?

Aladdin Us three!

Wishee }
Twanky } I'M OFF!!

Aladdin Come back here, you two! It's no good being afraid. You've got to think positive. Listen...

SONG
"HIGH HOPES"

Aladdin, Wishee *and* Twanky

Posed ending after song and dance. Over next lines **Surprise Surprise** *enters at back right, moves up behind them and exits at front right.*

Twanky This is a bit spooky, isn't it? I don't like it here. Can't we go inside the palace yet? Maybe there's some spooky moon people.

Aladdin There's no life on the moon! This talk of a man in the moon is just that! Talk!

Wishee I'm not too sure about that, but we are among friends, and if they see anything spooky, they'll let us know. You will, won't you?

Audience will now be yelling like mad. Usual ad-lib Who? What? Where? Behind us? Well; let's take a look. They circle round and as they go past exit **Surprise Surprise** *follows them, an arm hooks on to* **Wishee** *and he is dragged off unnoticed.* **Twanky** *and* **Aladdin** *return to front.*

Aladdin You must be mistaken, there's nothing here. But thanks for your help. If you DO see anything strange, do please let us know.

Twanky Oooh, yes, shout as loud as you can, won't you?

Surprise Surprise *returns and stays behind them.*

Twanky What is it?

Aladdin They seem really sure now, don't they? Let's have a good look this time. Let's try this way

116

As **Twanky** *and* **Aladdin** *go round,* **Surprise Surprise** *follows them round and drags* **Aladdin** *off.* **Twanky** *returns to front.*

Twanky You were wrong again. There was nothing there again.

Audience There was!!

Twanky Oh, no there wasn't.

Audience Oh, yes there was.

Twanky OH, NO THERE WASN'T.

Audience OH, YES THERE WAS.

Twanky Well, it's not there now. If you really do see something, then shout as loud as you possibly can, then I'll know about it straight away. Now, don't forget!!

Surprise Surprise *comes on and stays behind* **Twanky**. *Audience shouting.*

Twanky Now, are you sure this time? You're not kidding again, are you? Alright then, we'll have a look. You two go that way and I'll go this way.

She sets off round back, **Surprise Surprise** *follows. She comes back to front,* **Surprise Surprise** *stays behind her.*

No; there's nobody here except me and Wishee... *(looks to the side; he's not there)* ...er-er-m-m-me and A-A-Aladdin... *(She looks to other side; he's not there)*

117

Surprise Surprise *puts an arm on her shoulder, she looks at it and then at audience.*

Is this... er-er-*(points to it, turns, looks, screams and runs off fast)*

Surprise Surprise *(moves to front slowly and stops)* Nobody loves me!! *(turns to exit and repeats sadly)* Nobody loves ME! *(trudges off)*

Abanazer *enters and snarls in response to audience. He has the magic lamp tied to his belt.*

Abanazer Now is the time I have been waiting for. Very soon the Princess will be Mrs Abanazer, and you can all be the witnesses. *(claps)* Maidens!! Make the wedding place here. An ideal spot to tie the knot.

Sing Hi *and* **Sing Lo** *bring out low table with candles, and two cushions, which they place centre stage one at each side of table. They stay on stage.*

Abanazer *(to audience)* What say you now, you horrible horrors? *(boos)* Bah!! Spoilsports! Admit defeat, for you have lost! *(claps his hands)* Bring out some food for the wedding feast.

Sing Hi *moves to go off, but stops as* **Twanky** *comes on in a veil, carrying tray with goblets, wine and fruit bowl. She winks at audience, places tray on table.* **Abanazer** *takes no notice as she pours out wine, and shows packet marked clearly "SLEEPING POTION" to audience. She puts one tablet then another in* **Abanazer's** *goblet.*

118

Looks at him, then empties whole packet into goblet, and hands it to **Abanazer**.

Twanky Pray take the traditional pre-wedding drink, Your Eminence.

Abanazer A good idea! Bring the Princess.

> **Sing Lo** *goes to stage side,* **Princess** *enters crying.* **Abanazer** *notices* **Twanky**, *he hasn't had a drink yet.*

Abanazer *(to* **Twanky***)* Come here you. *(She does so nervously)* I haven't seen you before. Who are you?

Twanky I have been summoned by the Genie to assist at the wedding. Have a drink of wine, your Impotence.

Abanazer *(looks at lamp, then at* **Twanky***)* Let us see. We shall ask the Genie. *(takes hold of the lamp)*

Twanky That will not be necessary, Your Excellence. See, the Princess awaits! PLEASE, take a drink to prepare yourself for the wedding. This is a love potion!!

Abanazer Aha!! I see. *(gulps the wine.* **Twanky** *fans herself in relief)* Take your place, my dear. *(***Princess** *is crying)* AT ONCE!!

> *They kneel at opposite sides of table facing across the stage.* **Twanky** *looks in goblet, then at* **Abanazer**, *pretends to "time" him, looking at her wrist. She indicates "time up", he is still awake. She repeats this.*

Abanazer And now, my princess, we have come to the happy moment. Read the words on the card there. *(She cries)*

Come along, this is not going to be half as bad as you imagine. Read the card.

As she tries to read through card, **Twanky** *is still concerned about the potion.* **Aladdin** *enters at back with a large hammer with foam head, unnoticed by* **Abanazer.** **Aladdin** *comes behind him and indicates to audience "Shall I?" a couple of times.* **Aladdin** *is just about to strike* **Abanazer** *when* **Abanazer** *yawns and falls asleep.*

Princess Oh, Aladdin, thank goodness you are here! *(They embrace)*

Aladdin Everything is fine now. *(takes lamp from* **Abanazer's** *belt)* We have each other and we have the lamp!

Twanky Where's Wishee? WISHEE!!

Aladdin Wishee! You can come out now.

Wishee *enters at back with butterfly net, or similar comical weapon.*

Wishee HELLO, FOLKS!

Audience HELLO, WISHEE!

Wishee I'm ready for him. *(sweeps about with butterfly net and sees* **Abanazer)** Oh! What's up with him?

Twanky He's gone to sleep!

Wishee That's not very polite. What are we going to do with him? Are we going to leave him here, then there will be a man in the moon?

Abanazer *groans and starts to wake up.*

Abanazer What's happening? *(looks around and sees* **Aladdin***)* YOU!!

Aladdin Yes!! And I have the lamp.

Abanazer NO!! *(tries to get the lamp)*

Aladdin Oh, no you don't. *(threatens* **Abanazer** *with hammer)* *(to audience)* What shall we do with him?

They ad-lib to replies from the audience.

Twanky I rather fancy taking him back with me.

Abanazer NO!! NOT THAT!! I'd rather stay here on the moon!!

Aladdin We're not interested in what YOU want, but we'll have to make sure he doesn't cause us any more trouble.

Aladdin *rubs the lamp,* **Genie** *appears.*

Genie I am the Genie of the lamp. Your wish is my command, O Master.

Aladdin First of all, we must deal with this fellow. Remove all traces of wickedness from his soul so that we never have any trouble from him ever again.

Genie You command and I obey.

Abanazer Oh, no you don't!! I don't want to be good!

Genie *makes magical pass at* **Abanazer***, he freezes, puts his hands together and sings "Twinkle, Twinkle, little star", then hooks up with* **Twanky***.*

121

Aladdin Now, Genie, take all of us and the palace back to Peking, where we shall have our wedding before anything else goes wrong.

Princess Oh yes!! We will be so happy.

Genie Your wish is my command, O Master. Away we go TO PEKING!

They all cheer, wind noise as curtain closes.

End of Scene Nine

Scene Ten

COMMUNITY SONG

Wishee Washee *enters.*

Wishee HELLO, FOLKS!

Audience HELLO, WISHEE!!

Wishee It's great being back home. I didn't like it on the moon – no atmosphere, you know what I mean? You know, it's all happening back there – talk about weddings. There's Aladdin and the Princess, Prince Pekoe and Sing Hi, Mother and Abanazer, and guess what...? Me and Sing Lo. It's funny, she's been struggling for years to get a mink coat... then she gives up struggling and gets one straight away. Well now, it's your turn to do some work. It's Singa-longa-Wishee time. Can we have some words please*? (word cards from Scene Nine are thrown in)* Oh, ta very much. Now, can we have the right ones. **(Chop Suey** *and* **Chow Mein** *come on with the words)* Hey, it's them two, Chop Suey and Chow Mein. Come on chop, chop, chow, chow!! *(They sing it through)* Now, you all know the words. Right, ready, Maestro, after three... 6,7,8.

(after song) That was pretty good, not bad for starters.

Twanky *enters in gaudy dressing gown, ready to change for Finale.*

Twanky Pretty good? Not bad? I thought THAT side was terrible, didn't you? *(ad lib as sides sing against each other)*

Wishee *does last chorus on his own as* **Twanky** *goes to get changed.*

End of Scene Ten

FINALE

WALKDOWN

TOPICAL MUSIC

Chorus / Dancers

Surprise Surprise	**Fairy Diamante**
Genie / Executioner	**Vizir**
Chop Suey	**Chow Mein**

Emperor   Empress

Prince Pekoe and Sing Hi

Wishee Washee and Sing Lo

Abanazer

Widow Twanky

Aladdin and Princess

Music fades.

EMPRESS	Our pantomime is over
EMPEROR	We've done our very best
WISHEE	And now for you and all of us
TWANKY	It's time to have a rest
ABANAZER	The baddie's been defeated
GENIE	The goodie won the day
ALADDIN	So from Aladdin, the company
PRINCESS	and all of the crew
ALL	We'd just like to say "**HOORAY**"

TOPICAL FULL CHORUS SONG TO FINISH

Props List

ACT ONE

Scene One

Various stall items for opening scene

Executioner's oversized axe

Gong and hammer

Child's scooter

Imitation fire hose, about 10 feet long

Whistle

Water pistol

Small collection of laundry items, including a bra

Scene Two

Chinese fan

Laundry parcels

Placards with handles. One says (from top to bottom):

> GET
> YOUR
> CHICKEN

The other says:

> STUFFED
> FOWL
> HEAD

(Amusing when they stand side by side)

Proclamation (scroll)

Two starting pistols firing blanks (or two mock pistols and sound effects)

Scene Three

Money pouch

Laundry items, washing powder packet, tubs for the "production line"

Cardboard cut-out long johns

Washing on a rope wound round Twanky's waist to reveal as she spins around in "Stripper"

Two buckets (with water/goo?)

Bowler hat with shaving foam in and a hole in the top

Towels

(Wicker) basket to catch Aladdin's head

Scene Four

Two plastic skulls, one small and one larger

Magic trick

Magic ring

Scene Five

The magic lamp

Tray, glasses, bottle of (Lucozade?)

Boxes of jewels, jewels revealed on the stage in magical fashion

Treasure chest

ACT TWO

Scene Six

> "Magical" cut-out palace to be flown in/revealed at back of stage
>
> Loose jewels
>
> (Beer) bottle

Scene Seven

> Table and seating for five
>
> Magic trick
>
> Tray, teapot, cups, sugar bowl, saucers etc
>
> Display prop of "newer" lamps

Scene Eight

> Bench
>
> Rings (Olympic style) for fairy dance
>
> Tardis front (with practical door)

Scene Nine

> Cardboard, foil covered space helmets, oxygen tanks etc (easily removed)
>
> Cards with words written on, clearly visible to audience
>
> Low table, "candles", cushions
>
> Tray with goblets, wine, fruit bowl
>
> Packet marked clearly "SLEEPING POTION"
>
> Large hammer with foam head
>
> Butterfly net

Printed in Great Britain
by Amazon

57150948R00076